## Smithsonian Report.

ON THE

# CONSTRUCTION

OF

# CATALOGUES OF LIBRARIES,

AND THEIR

## PUBLICATION BY MEANS OF SEPARATE, STEREOTYPED TITLES.

WITH RULES AND EXAMPLES.

BY CHARLES C. JEWETT,

LIBRARIAN OF THE SMITHSONIAN INSTITUTION.

SECOND EDITION.

WASHINGTON:

PUBLISHED BY THE SMITHSONIAN INSTITUTION.

1853.

STEREOTYPED AND PRINTED AT THE
SMITHSONIAN INSTITUTION.

# CONTENTS.


| | Page. |
|---|---|
| PREFACE, | v |
| REPORT OF COMMISSIONERS, | ix |
| **SMITHSONIAN CATALOGUE SYSTEM.** | |
| Difficulties in publishing catalogues, | 3 |
| Plan for obviating these difficulties, | 5 |
| Application of the plan for the formation of a general catalogue, | 5 |
| Advantages to be derived from the proposed system, | 6 |
| Distinction between a catalogue and a bibliographical dictionary, | 10 |
| The same titles to serve for general and particular catalogues, | 11 |
| Form of the catalogue, | 13 |
| Necessity of rules for the preparation of catalogues, | 17 |
| Duties of collaborators and superintendent, | 19 |
| Printing and Stereotyping, | 23 |
| Preservation and use of the plates, | 24 |
| Construction of new catalogues, | 25 |
| **RULES.** | |
| Titles. | |
| I. To be transcribed IN FULL, | 29 |
| II. To be transcribed WITH EXACTNESS, | 31 |
| III. To be repeated for every edition, | 34 |
| IV. Books without title-pages, | 35 |
| V. Academical dissertations, | 36 |
| VI. Sermons, | 36 |
| VII. Periodical publications, | 36 |
| VIII. Number of volumes, how to be specified, | 37 |
| IX. Imprint, | 38 |
| X. Designation of size, | 39 |
| XI. Number of pages, | 43 |
| XII. Additions to titles, | 44 |

HEADINGS.

XIII. To be, generally, the name of author, . . . . 45
XIV. Names variously spelled, . . . . . . 46
XV. Prefixes to names, . . . . . . 46
XVI. Compound surnames, . . . . . . 48
XVII. Names changed, . . . . . . . 48
XVIII. Cases in which the first name is to be used, . . 49
XIX. Surnames of noblemen, &c., . . . . . 50
XX. Joint productions of several authors, . . . . 50
XXI. Works of several authors in one series, . . . 50
XXII. Works issued by collective bodies, . . . . 52
XXIII. Translations, . . . . . . . 53
XXIV. Commentaries, . . . . . . . 53
XXV. The Bible, . . . . . . . 54
XXVI. Reports of Trials, . . . . . . . 54
XXVII. Theses, . . . . . . . . 54
XXVIII. Pseudonymous publications, . . . . . 54
XXIX. Anonymous publications, . . . . . 55

CROSS-REFERENCES.

XXX. From one heading to another, . . . . . 57
XXXI. From headings to titles, . . . . 58

ARRANGEMENT.

XXXII. Order of headings, . . . . . . . 59
XXXIII. Order of titles, . . . . . . . 59
XXXIV. Order of titles under name of author, . . . . 60
1. Collection of all the works, . . . . . 60
a. Without translations, . . . . . . 60
b. With one, or several translations, . . . . 60
c. Translations without the text, . . . . 60
2. Partial collections, . . . . . . 60
3. Selections, or collected fragments, . . . . 60
4. Separate works, . . . . . . 61
5. Entire portions of a separate work, . . . . 61
XXXV. Order of titles under names of collective bodies, . . 61
XXXVI. Cross-references, . . . . . . . 61
XXXVII. Special rule for entries under "Bible," . . . . 61
XXXVIII. Maps, Engravings, Music, . . . . . . 62
XXXIX. Exceptional cases, . . . . . . 64

EXAMPLES.

# PREFACE.

This work is intended to explain the plan in operation at the Smithsonian Institution, for preparing and stereotyping catalogues; to furnish means of judging of its practicability and importance; and to serve as a a manual for librarians in its execution. The first edition was printed in 1852. It was, however, limited to a small number of copies, for distribution principally among those who would be likely to suggest improvements. The work has, since, been carefully revised, and is now published for more general circulation.

It was a long and difficult task to develop and adjust the details of this system, and to make the mechanical arrangements for its successful prosecution. The difficulties, both theoretical and practical, have been overcome. The actual operation of the plan has shown its entire practicability, and warrants the hope that its best promises will be realized.

This book has been stereotyped by a process entirely new, peculiarly adapted to the stereotyping of separate titles, or even single lines. It has been fully reduced to practice for this special purpose, and will doubtless be found, in many other respects, a valuable addition to the resources of the art of typography.

The expense of developing the plan has been borne by the Smithsonian Institution. We have every reason to hope that it will promote "the increase and diffusion of knowledge among men," and justify the continual labor of superintendence. In anticipation, the task proposed seems formidable; but it is to be accomplished, *title by title*, on a system, which imposes no heavy burden upon any institution, though it offers benefits to all.

It is not to be supposed that the public will take much interest in a work of professional details like this. The subject more particularly addresses itself to those who are conversant with the management of libraries. Their instruction and experience will enable them to estimate aright the difficulty of the undertaking here set forth, and to judge, with fairness, of its practical utility.

# REPORT.

# COPY OF A LETTER

Addressed severally to the Hon. EDWARD EVERETT, of Cambridge; CHARLES FOLSOM, esq., Librarian of the Boston Athenæum; JOSEPH G. COGSWELL, esq., Superintendent of the Astor Library, New York; GEORGE LIVERMORE, esq., of Boston; SAMUEL F. HAVEN, esq., Librarian of the American Antiquarian Society, and the Rev. EDWARD E. HALE, of Worcester.

---

SMITHSONIAN INSTITUTION,
*August* 16, 1850.

DEAR SIR: The Smithsonian Institution, desirous of facilitating research in literature and science, and of thus aiding in the increase and diffusion of knowledge, has resolved to form a general catalogue of the various libraries in the United States, and I submit to you for examination the plans proposed by Professor Jewett, librarian of the Institution, for accomplishing this object.

1st. A plan for stereotyping catalogues of libraries by separate titles, in a uniform style.

2d. A set of general rules, to be recommended for adoption by the different libraries of the United States, in the preparation of their catalogues.

Professor Jewett will present to you his plans in person, and I beg leave, in behalf of the Executive Committee of the Institution, to request that you will give this subject that attention which its importance demands, and report:

First. On the practicability of the plan presented.

Second. On the propriety of adopting the rules proposed.

You will also confer a favor on the Institution, by giving any suggestions with regard to the general proposition of forming a catalogue of all the libraries in this country.

I remain respectfully, your obedient servant,

JOSEPH HENRY,
*Secretary of the Smithsonian Institution.*

# REPORT

*Of the Commissioners appointed to examine the plan for forming a general stereotype catalogue of public libraries in the United States.*

---

The undersigned were requested, in the month of August last, by a letter from Professor Henry, written on behalf of the Executive Committee of the Smithsonian Institution, to take into consideration the subject of a General Catalogue of the public libraries of the United States, proposed to be formed under the auspices of the said Institution, and more especially the plan proposed by Professor Jewett, Librarian of the Institution, for accomplishing that object.

Having consented to act as Commissioners for the above named purpose, the subscribers had several interviews with Professor Jewett, in the months of September and October, at which he submitted to them, 1. A plan for stereotyping catalogues of libraries by separate, movable titles of the books contained in them, and, 2. A set of general rules, to be recommended for adoption by the different public libraries in the United States, in the preparation of their catalogues.

Professor Jewett's plan for stereotyping titles on separate plates is unfolded at considerable length, in a paper read by him, in the month of August last, at the annual meeting of the American Association for the Advancement of Science, held at New Haven.

For a full view of the advantages, both economical and literary, anticipated from the adoption of Professor Jewett's plan, the undersigned would refer to the valuable and interesting paper just named. They will allude briefly to a portion of these advantages.

The most important of them, perhaps, will be the economy of time, labor, and expense, required for the preparation of a new edition of a catalogue, to include the books added since a former edition was published. On Professor Jewett's plan, when the catalogue of a library is published, it will be necessary to strike off only so many copies as are needed for present use. When the additions to the library have become so considerable as to make another edition of the catalogue desirable, or in lieu thereof, a supplementary catalogue, (always an unsatisfactory and embarrassing appendage,) the new titles only will be stereotyped and inserted in their proper places among the former titles, all the titles being on movable plates. The pages of the new edition will thus be made up with convenience, and every book in the library will stand in its proper place in the catalogue. This process will be repeated as often as the growth of the library may make it necessary.

In this way, not only will the plates, used in a former edition, be available for each subsequent edition, but when the plan is fairly and extensively in operation, most of the titles of books added to any given library, of whose catalogue a new edition is required, will, in the meantime, have been cast for some other catalogue, and thus occasion no new charge for any subsequent use, as far as the expense of casting the plates is concerned. The infant state and the prospective rapid increase of the public libraries in the United States, as well as the frequent founding of new libraries, give great interest to this feature of the plan.

Another advantage of the proposed plan would be of the following nature: The libraries in any country, (to some extent, indeed, in all countries,) consist partly of the same books. Professor Jewett states that, in the catalogues of public libraries of the United States, possessed by the Smithsonian Institution, there are embraced at least four hundred and fifty thousand titles. He estimates, however, after a laborious comparison, that among these there will not be found more than one hundred and fifty thousand different titles. It follows, that if the plan proposed had been applied to the publication of these catalogues, two-thirds of the expense of printing them, as far as the cost of plates is concerned, would have been saved, by incurring the extra expense of stereotyping the remaining third according to this plan. The economy to each particular library, in the expense of plates for its catalogue, will be in proportion to the number of books, which it may contain in common with any other library, whose catalogue has been already stereotyped on this plan. The title of the same book, in the same edition, will, of course, be cast but once, and will thenceforward serve for the catalogue of every library possessing that book, which may enter into the arrangement.

A third advantage resulting from this plan will be the facility, with which a *classed* catalogue, either of a whole library or of any department of it, might be furnished at short notice, without the expense of writing out the titles, or of casting new plates, but by the simple indication of the selected titles, in the margin of a printed alphabetical catalogue.

Finally, the plan of necessity requires that the titles of the books in the libraries, included in the arrangement, should be given on uniform principles, and according to fixed rules; an object of no small importance to those who consult them.

These and other incidental advantages, which would result from the adoption of his plan of separate stereotype plates, for the titles of books in public libraries, are pointed out by Professor Jewett in the memoir above referred to, and the undersigned are of opinion that he has not overrated their importance. In proportion as the plan is concurred in by the public institutions and individuals possessing valuable collections of books, the preparation of a general catalogue of all the libraries in the country becomes practicable, accompanied by references from which it would appear in what library or libraries any particular book is contained.

The undersigned became satisfied, in the course of their conferences with Professor Jewett, that the plan in all its parts is practicable. In connection with the explanation of its mechanical execution, specimens of stereotype plates of separate titles, made up into pages, were submitted to them, in common type metal, in electrotype, and in a newly-invented composition, the use of which, it is thought by its inventor, would be attended with great economy in the cost of plates. The undersigned examined these specimens with much gratification and interest, but they did not feel themselves competent, from their limited opportunities of inquiry, nor did they regard it as falling within their province, to form an opinion on the comparative merits of these processes. They feel satisfied that no important mechanical difficulty is to be apprehended in carrying the plan into full effect.

A majority of the undersigned devoted themselves for several successive meetings to the careful consideration of the set of rules, submitted to them by Professor Jewett, for the uniform preparation of the titles of books. This is a subject which has of late received much attention from bibliographers, and is of great importance in the formation of the catalogues of public libraries. Professor Jewett's rules combine the results of the experience of those who have given their attention to the subject in the principal libraries of Europe, especially of the British Museum, together with the fruits of his own experience and study. These rules appear to the undersigned to be drawn up with judgment and care. A few amendments were recommended by the undersigned, and a few additions proposed, but they are prepared to signify their approval of the system substantially as submitted to them.

In order that a beginning may be made in the execution of the plan, under circumstances highly favorable to its success, the undersigned take the liberty of suggesting, that it would be advisable for the Regents of the Smithsonian Institution to obtain the requisite authority, to prepare a catalogue of the library of Congress on the above-described plan. A catalogue of this library is now very much wanted. Originally constructed on a defective plan, and continued by the publication of a large number of supplements, it is now almost useless; and as the library increases, it becomes daily more so. The preparation of an alphabetical catalogue has in this way become a matter of absolute necessity for the library itself; while it affords the best opportunity for commencing an arrangement, by which the various libraries of the country will be brought into a mutually beneficial connexion with each other, on the plan proposed by Professor Jewett.

The undersigned consider the permanent superintendence of this plan to be an object entirely within the province of the Smithsonian Institution. They are satisfied that it will tend both to the increase and diffusion of knowledge, and they therefore hope, that the sanction of the Regents and of Congress will be given to the undertaking.

(Signed,)

EDWARD EVERETT,
JOSEPH G. COGSWELL,
CHARLES FOLSOM,
SAMUEL F. HAVEN,
EDWARD E. HALE,
GEORGE LIVERMORE.

BOSTON, 26th October, 1850.

# SYSTEM.

# SMITHSONIAN CATALOGUE SYSTEM.

## DIFFICULTIES IN PUBLISHING CATALOGUES.

Few persons, except librarians, are aware of the nature and extent of the difficulties, which have been encountered, in attempting to furnish suitable printed catalogues of growing libraries; difficulties apparently insurmountable, and menacing a common abandonment of the hope of affording guides, so important, to the literary accumulations of the larger libraries of Europe.

It is, of course, entirely practicable to publish a complete and satisfactory catalogue of a library which is stationary. But most public libraries are constantly and rapidly increasing. This circumstance, so gratifying on every other account, is the source of the difficulties alluded to.

While the catalogue of such a library is passing through the press, new books are received, the titles of which it is impossible, in the ordinary manner of printing, to incorporate with the body of the work. Recourse must then be had to a supplement. In no other way can the acquisitions of the library be made known to the the public. If the number of supplements be multiplied, as they have been in the library of Congress, the student may be obliged to grope his weary way through ten catalogues, instead of one, in order to ascertain whether the book which he seeks be in the library. He cannot be certain, even then, that the book is not in the collection, for it may have been received, since the last appendix was printed. Supplements soon become intolerable. The whole catalogue must then be re-arranged and re-printed. The expense of this process may be borne, so long as the library is small, but it soon becomes burdensome, and, ere long, insupportable, even to national establishments.

There is but one course left—not to print at all. To this no scholar consents, except from necessity. But to this alternative, grievous as it is, nearly all the large libraries of Europe have been reluctantly driven.

More than a century has passed, since the printing of the catalogue of the Royal Library at Paris was commenced. It is not yet finished. No one feels in it the interest which he would, if he could hope to have its completeness sustained, when once brought up to a given date.

Dr. Pertz, chief librarian of the Royal Library at Berlin, declares, that to print the catalogue of a large library, which is constantly increasing, is to throw away money. His opinion is founded upon the supposed impossibility of keeping up the catalogue, so as continually to represent the actual possessions of the library.

The commissioners, lately appointed by the Queen of England, to inquire into the constitution and management of the British Museum, have, in their report, expressed an opinion decidedly against the printing of the catalogue at all, and principally on the ground that it must ever remain imperfect.

One of the witnesses, (the Right Honorable J. W. Croker,) examined before the commissioners, thus strongly states the case with respect to printing:

"You receive, I suppose, into your library every year some twenty thousand volumes, or something like that. Why, if you had a printed catalogue dropped down from Heaven to you at this moment perfect, this day twelve-month your twenty thousand interlineations would spoil the simplicity of that catalogue; again the next year twenty thousand more; and the next year twenty thousand more; so that at the end of four or five years, you would have your catalogue just in the condition that your new catalogue is now [the manuscript part greater than the printed part]. With that new catalogue before your eyes, I am astonished that there should be any discussion about it, for there is the experiment; the experiment has been made and failed."

Not one European library, of the first class, has a complete printed catalogue, in a single work. The Bodleian Library is not an exception. It may be necessary to search six distinct catalogues, in order to ascertain whether any specified book were or were not in that collection, at the close of the year 1847.

This is, surely, a disheartening state of things. It has been felt and lamented by every one who has had the care of an increasing library.

### PLAN FOR OBVIATING THESE DIFFICULTIES.

As a remedy for this evil, it is proposed to **STEREOTYPE THE TITLES SEPARATELY**, and to preserve the plates or blocks, in alphabetical order of the titles, so as to be able readily to insert additional titles, in their proper places, and then to reprint the whole catalogue. By these means, the chief cost of re-publication (that of composition) together with the trouble of revision and correction of the press, would, except for new titles, be avoided. Some of the great difficulties, which have so long oppressed and discouraged librarians, and involved libraries in enormous expenses, may be thus overcome.

### APPLICATION OF THE PLAN TO THE FORMATION OF A GENERAL CATALOGUE.

The peculiar position of the Smithsonian Institution suggested the application of this plan, on a wider scale, and for a more important purpose, than that of merely facilitating the publication of new and complete editions of separate catalogues.

It had been proposed to form a general catalogue of all the books in the country, with references to the libraries where each might be found. The plan of stereotyping titles, separately, suggested the following system for the accomplishment of this important purpose:

1. The Smithsonian Institution to publish Rules for the preparation of Catalogues.

2. Other institutions, intending to publish catalogues of their books, to be requested to prepare them in accordance with these rules, with a view to their being stereotyped under the direction of the Smithsonian Institution.

3. The Smithsonian Institution to pay the whole *extra* expense of stereotyping, or such part thereof as may be agreed on.

4. The stereotyped titles to remain the property of the Smithsonian Institution.

5. Every library, acceding to this plan, to have the right of using all the titles in the possession of the Institution, as often as desired, for the printing of its own catalogue, by the Smithsonian Institution; paying only the expense of making up the pages, of press-work, and of distributing the titles to their proper places.

6. The Smithsonian Institution to publish, as soon as possible, and at stated intervals, a General Catalogue of all Libraries coming into this system.

## ADVANTAGES TO BE DERIVED FROM THIS SYSTEM OF PREPARING CATALOGUES.

The plan of stereotyping the titles, separately, would be of great value to every increasing library, independent of any general system. Such a library, in the first issue of its catalogue, would be obliged to incur an additional expense for stereotyping, which we may, for the present, state at fifty per centum above the price for composition. But, in the first reprint, both these expenses would be saved; so that the whole cost of the two editions would, in this respect, be twenty-five per cent. less, if stereotyped.

Moreover, it would be necessary to print only a comparatively small number of copies, when the book, in a more perfect state, could be reproduced so easily; much would therefore be saved in paper and press-work. Besides, the arrangement of the titles, for a reprint, would pass from the hands of the librarian to those of the printer. The proof-reading, also, would have been done, once for all. In keeping up such a catalogue, the attention and labor of the librarian would have to be bestowed only upon additional titles.

Reckoning, thus, the expense of stereotyping as a part of the diminished cost of the first reprint, the saving, for every subsequent repetition, would be equal to the whole original cost of composition and proof-reading, for the part already stereotyped, and a considerable part of that of paper, press-work, and rearrangement. It is, therefore, demonstrable that the economy of the plan would be very great, to every library publishing and reprinting its catalogues, even without connection with the system proposed.

But, in connection with a general system, the advantages of this plan would be greatly increased, inasmuch as the same books are to be found in many libraries. If the titles, which have been stereotyped for one library, may be used for another having the same books, the saving to the second would be equal to the whole cost of composition and stereotyping of the titles common to the two, added to that of preparation of such titles.

At least one quarter of the titles in any two general libraries, of ten thousand volumes and upwards, may safely be supposed to be the same. The saving, from this source, to the second library, would, therefore, go far towards defraying the extra expense of stereotyping. A third institution, adopting the plan, would be likely to find a very large proportion of its titles identical with those already stereotyped, and the amount saved by the use of these titles, would, perhaps, be sufficient to counterbalance the whole extra expenditure for stereotyping. At any rate, the extra expense would be constantly and rapidly diminishing, and would, probably after the fourth or fifth catalogue, cease entirely. The Smithsonian Institution would not, therefore, be required to assume the charge of an enterprise, which might involve it in great and increasing expense, but merely to organize, and to guide a system, which will almost immediately pay its own way, and will soon save large sums of money to our public libraries.

That the aggregate economy of this plan would be very great, may be seen from the following statement:

In fifteen thousand pages, mostly in octavo, of catalogues of public libraries in the United States, there were found to be more than four hundred and fifty thousand titles. But, according to the best estimate which could be made, these catalogues contained not more than one hundred and fifty thousand *different* titles. Two-thirds, at least, of the whole cost of printing these catalogues (except the extra expense incurred by stereotyping the titles which differed) might have been saved, by following this plan.

Having shown its economy when employed by single libraries, and its greater economy, in connection with a general system, it is proper to suggest a few, among the many benefits to the cause of knowledge, which the general adoption of this method would seem to promise.

It can hardly be necessary to dwell, at length, upon the benefits to be expected from a general printed catalogue of all books in the public libraries of America. By means of it, every student in this country would be able to learn the full extent of his resources for investigation. The places where books could be found, might be indicated in the catalogue. A correspondence could be kept up between this Institution and every other library in the country. A system of exchange and of loans might, with certain stringent conditions, be established, or, when the loan of a book would be impracticable, extracts could be copied, quotations verified, and researches made, through the intervention of this Institution, as effectually to the purpose of the student, in most cases, as a personal examination of the book. All the literary treasures of the country might thus be made measurably available to every scholar.

Again, this general catalogue would enable purchasers of books for public libraries, to consult judiciously for the wants of the country. So poor are we in the books which scholars need; so long, at best, must we remain in a condition of provincial dependence in literary matters; that a responsibility to the whole country rests upon the man, who selects books for any public library.

An important advantage of this system is, that it allows us to vary the form of the catalogue, at will, from the alphabetical to the classed, and to modify the classification as we please. The titles, separately stereotyped, may change their order at command. If, for example, it were required to print a separate list of all books in the country, on the subject of *meteorology*, it would merely be necessary to check off, in the general catalogue, the titles to be used, leaving to the printer the rest of the work.

Another highly beneficial result would be, the attainment of a much higher degree of *uniformity* than could otherwise be hoped for. The rules for cataloguing must be stringent, and should meet, as far as possible, all difficulties of detail. Nothing, so far as can be avoided, should be left to the individual taste or judgment of the cataloguer. He should be a man of sufficient learning, accuracy and fidelity, to apply the rules. In cases of doubt, reference should be made to the central establishment, to which the whole work should be submitted, page by page, for examination and revision. Thus, we should have all our catalogues formed substantially on one plan. Now, even if the one adopted were that of the worst of our catalogues, if it were strictly followed in all alike, their uniformity would render catalogues, thus made, far more useful than the present chaos of irregularities. The best possible system ought, however, to be the object of our aim.

It is an important consideration, that this plan would greatly facilitate the formation of an American bibliography, or a complete account of all books published in America.

By law, a copy of every book, for which a copyright shall be secured, in this country, is required to be delivered to the Smithsonian Institution, and to be preserved therein. It is hoped, that additional legislation, on this subject, will soon lighten the burdens of publishers, and secure the observance of this law, *in all cases*.

The collection of books thus obtained and preserved, will present a complete monumental history of American literature, during the existence of the law. It is needless to enlarge upon its value, in this point of view. If, now, a list of these publications, as they come into the library, should, month by month, be published in a *Bulletin*, and the titles immediately stereotyped, the expense would be but trifling of issuing, every year, a catalogue of books copyrighted in America, during the year, and printing, every five years, a general catalogue of American publications, up to that limit. Thus, monthly bulletins, annual lists, and quinquennial catalogues would furnish full and satisfactory records of American publications.

Another general consideration is, that this project looks towards the accomplishment of that cherished dream of scholars, *a universal catalogue*. If the system should be successful, in this country, it may eventually be so in every country of Europe. When all shall have adopted and carried out the plan, each for itself, the aggregate of general catalogues, thus formed—few in number—will embrace the whole body of literature extant, and from them, it will be no impossible task to digest and publish a universal bibliography. How much this would promote the progress of knowledge, by showing, more distinctly, what has been attempted and accomplished, and what yet remains to be achieved, and thus indicating the path of useful effort; how much, by rebuking the rashness which rushes into authorship, ignorant of what others have written, and adding to the mass of books, without adding to the sum of knowledge; how much, by giving confidence to the true and heroic student, who fears no labor, so that it bring him to the height at which he aims—the summit of learning, in the branch to which he devotes himself; are objects which deserve the hopeful attention of all who desire their attainment.

## DISTINCTION BETWEEN A CATALOGUE AND A BIBLIOGRAPHICAL DICTIONARY.

A catalogue of a library is, strictly speaking, but a list of the titles of the books, which it contains. It is not generally expected to give any further description of a book than the author gives, or ought to give in the title-page, and the publisher, in the imprint, or colophon; except the designation of form, which is, almost universally, added.

A bibliographical dictionary is supposed to contain, besides the titles of books, such descriptions, more or less extended, drawn from all available sources of information, as may be necessary to furnish means of identifying each work, of distinguishing its different editions, of ascertaining the requisites of a perfect copy, of learning all facts of interest respecting its authorship, publication, typography, subsequent casualties, alterations, etc., its market value, and the estimation in which it is held.

A catalogue is designed to show what books are contained in a particular collection, and nothing more. Persons in want of further information, are expected to seek for it in bibliographical dictionaries, literary histories, or similar works.

Inasmuch, however, as bibliographical works are not always accessible, or known to the investigator, additions are, not unfrequently, made to the titles, in catalogues, of such notices as belong more appropriately to bibliographical dictionaries, as above described. These, of course, impart to such catalogues greater value and usefulness.

As bibliographers, we cannot indeed but wish, that the catalogue of every library were a bibliographical dictionary of its books.

Practically, however, we must restrict our efforts, within the limits of probable accomplishment. There is no species of literary labor so arduous, or which makes so extensive demands upon the learning of the author, as that of the preparation of such works. The most which one man can hope to effect, in this department, is to examine and describe books, in some special branch of knowledge, or books of some particular class, as *palæotypes*, books privately printed, a selection of books most esteemed by collectors, &c. It is too much to expect, that every librarian can find time, or possess learning, for such a description of all books under his care. Besides, this would be a waste of labor and of money. The same description would be prepared and printed, a hundred or a thousand times.

It is doubtless desirable, that such results of *original* investigations of librarians, as are not to be found in any of the bibliographical dictionaries, should be given, in the catalogues which they publish. In other cases, also, as will appear hereafter, it may be important to give, in a catalogue, fuller and more accurate descriptions of books, than are to be found upon their title-pages; but the principle should be established, and ever borne in mind, that a catalogue, being designed to be merely a list of titles, with imprints and designations of size, all additional descriptions should be limited and regulated by explicit rules, in order to give uniformity and system to the work, and to restrict its bulk and cost, within reasonable bounds.

## PREPARATION OF TITLES SO AS TO SERVE FOR BOTH GENERAL AND PARTICULAR CATALOGUES.

It is proposed to prepare and stereotype catalogues of particular libraries, in such a manner, that the titles can be used, without alteration, for constructing a General Catalogue.

This requires, that the title of every book be such, as will apply to every copy of the same edition.

If the edition be different, the book is to be considered different. In almost every instance, the title also, is different. There are, indeed, cases, where the title of a book is the same, in two editions, while the body of the work is more or less altered. Such instances are, however, of rare occurrence. They are, or should be, recorded in bibliographical works. They could only be described by one, who should place the two books side by side, and compare them together. In general, titles vary with the editions. We may, therefore, in using a title transcribed from one copy of a book, for other copies, avoid trouble by preparing and stereotyping a new title for every distinct edition; treating new editions as new books. So that, if copies of various editions of a work exist in several libraries, each will appear with a distinct title, in the General Catalogue.

This method of forming a general catalogue requires, further, that *peculiarities of copy*, which it may be desirable to note in preparing the catalogues of particular libraries, should not be stated within the titles; but, if at all, in notes appended to the titles, and entirely separate from them.

One copy of the same edition of a book may be on vellum, another, on paper; one may be in quarto form, another in octavo; one may have cancelled leaves, another, the substituted leaves, another, added leaves; some may contain autographs; some, valuable manuscript notes; others may be bound by Roger Payne, etc., etc. These are peculiarities of copy, and they may be as numerous as the number of copies in the edition. They are not noticed in title-pages, and, consequently, would not modify the entries in a catalogue, which takes cognizance of titles alone.

The printed matter, which constitutes the book, as a literary production, is not altered, in any of these cases, except in that of cancelled, substituted, or added leaves. It is indeed true, that, occasionally, alterations are made in the body of a book, while it is passing through the press: that is to say, after a few copies have been struck off, some error may be discovered and corrected, or some word may be substituted for another. But, such changes are always slight, and can only be detected, by comparing two or more copies of a work together. In the case of cancelled leaves, it may, sometimes be desirable to print in the general catalogue, the description of rare and important copies possessed by particular libraries. But these cases would occur comparatively seldom. The rule would be, to omit from the title to be stereotyped, all account of peculiarities, or defects of copies.

In cataloguing particular libraries, such peculiarities should be stated, upon the card, after the title, but separate from it. They may be printed, at the expense of such libraries, in the form of notes to their catalogues. The notes for any particular library may be made as extensive, as the means of the institution, and the learning and leisure of its librarian permit.

There is another particular, in which the catalogue title might vary, in different copies: that, of designation of size. The same book, in the same edition, may have copies in quarto, in octavo, and in duodecimo. The size of the printed page is, however, in all these cases, the same; otherwise, the edition is different. All difficulty, on this account, therefore, is obviated, and all confusion of editions prevented, by adopting, instead of, or in addition to the usual designation of *form*, as the indication of size, the measurement of the printed page, in inches and tenths. Other reasons for this mode of marking the size of books, with minute directions, will be given hereafter.

## FORM OF THE CATALOGUE.

The titles constituting the catalogue may be variously arranged. They may be placed under the names of authors, and the names disposed in alphabetical order; they may be grouped in classes, according to subjects; or they may be made to follow the order of the date, or place of printing.

The two most common forms for catalogues, are the alphabetical and the classed. Much controversy has arisen respecting their comparative usefulness. It is not necessary to revive it here, since the system now proposed, renders it easy to vary the order of titles, so as to suit any desired form.

For the General Catalogue, however, it is, for several reasons, desirable to adopt the alphabetical arrangement.

It would be impossible to propose any system of classification, which would command general approval, or upon which a commission of competent bibliographers would be unanimous in opinion.

A classification, founded upon the nature of things, though it has occupied the best thoughts of such men as Bacon, Leibnitz, D'Alembert, Coleridge, Ampère, and many others, has not yet been attained. Every classification which has been proposed or used, is more or less arbitrary, and consequently unsatisfactory, and liable to be altered or superseded.

If, however, it were possible to agree upon a system of classification, the attempt to carry it out would, in a work like that proposed, be fatal to uniformity. Where different men were applying the same system, their opinions would vary, with their varying intelligence and skill. This would lead to utter and irremediable confusion, and would eventually defeat all our plans.

Even were these objections obviated, the occurrence of fewer difficulties in constructing an alphabetical catalogue would still present a decisive argument in its favor. Even these are great. If increased, by an attempt at classification, they would soon lead to an abandonment of the work.

Another consideration of great weight is, that, in reprinting classified catalogues, and inserting additions, if the titles were kept in systematic order, the work of selecting those to be used, and of distributing them to their places, would have to be done by a person, who, besides being a practical printer, should be familiar with the bibliographical system adopted. This would be very expensive. Whereas, on the alphabetical plan, any printer could do the whole.

On general considerations, without special reference to those which are peculiar to this system of publishing, alphabetical catalogues are to be preferred;—catalogues in which all the works of each author are placed under his name, and the names of authors are arranged alphabetically; anonymous works being entered under the first word of the title, not an article or preposition. Such is now the general opinion of competent bibliographers and literary men.

The Edinburgh Review, in an able and interesting article upon the British Museum, holds the following language:

"It seems to have been almost universally agreed that the catalogue ought to be alphabetical. Some time ago the current of opinion among literary men seemed to be setting towards classed catalogues, or those in which the books are arranged according to subjects. We had hardly supposed that this illusion (as we hold it to be) had become so nearly obsolete as the evidence before us shows that it is: and this disappearance of a most injurious opinion, which never was entertained to any extent by the really experienced in bibliography, encourages us to hope that it will not be long before the *professional* persons just alluded to [librarians] will be admitted to know best on all the points which have been raised relative to the care of a large library."

The experience of all students, of all who use books, if carefully noted, will show, that, in a vast majority of cases, whoever wishes to refer to books in a library, knows the names of their authors. It follows, that this form of arrangement must be, in the main, the most convenient; and if any other be pursued, it can but accommodate the minority, at the expense of the majority.

Still, it is indisputable that, oftentimes, the names of authors are not known; that one knows, merely, what subjects he wishes to investigate.

It may be said, that a catalogue, being designed to be merely a list of books contained in a library, is not to be expected to furnish this information; and that references to all authors, treating of any particular subjects, may be obtained from bibliographical works, encyclopædias, and other sources of information. This is true. But, unfortunately, these sources of information are not generally known, or not readily accessible, even to men of considerable attainments and scholarship.

It becomes, then, a question of importance how far the wants of such persons are to be provided for. The following remarks on this subject are worthy of attentive consideration:

"On this, as on other points, we may observe that two descriptions of persons consult a catalogue—those who know *precisely* what book they are in search of, and those who do not. The first will find by any rule, so soon as they have learnt it; and will be glad indeed of a catalogue which preserves its consistency, even though 600,000 titles, running over four quarters of the globe, four centuries of time, and four hundred varieties of usage, should actually require *ninety-one** rules of digestion. The second class could easily

*These are not all that might be wanted. For example, the case is not provided for, though it has occurred, in which an author, in his title-page, invites the reader to make his choice between two ways of spelling his own name. Here, we are to presume, some of our witnesses would take the first method given, others would leave the cataloguer to comply with the author's request.

be suited, if all their imperfect conceptions tended to the same case of confusion: and, as being the majority, would have a right to the adoption of the one nearly universal misconception; which, being one, would furnish a rule. But it is truth which is single, while error is manifold; and consequently, it is clear to every common sense except that of men of letters claiming, as such, to be bibliographers, that one of two things should be done:—either the truth should be taken, when known, or in the event of it being possible to be wrong, the error should be the consequence of a digested and easily-apprehended rule, consistently applied throughout. If the framer of the catalogue be allowed to do as he likes, the consulter of it must do as he can. Now which of the two classes should be considered in preference,—those who know what they want or those who do not? The Doctor of Divinity already quoted, gives this as one of his rules: 'Item, whan anie man comith and wotteth not what he wold haue, then he (the keper of the Bokys) shall tell hym, and doe hym to understond hys besynesse.' This can be done, to a certain extent, by *cross-references*. But, all cross-references being concessions to want of accurate knowledge, it is plain that discretionary entries, with discretionary cross-references, would form a plan which puts entirely out of the question the convenience of the person who knows exactly what he wants; which kills both calf and cow for the less deserving son, without giving the power of making any answer to the complaint of the one who never fed on husks. Nothing is stranger in the course of the evidence before us, than the quiet manner in which the opponents of the existing plan take it for granted that no one ever goes with a precise knowledge of the title-page of the work he seeks, unless it be the coolness with which this accurate inquirer is told, as Mr. Carlyle said to those who write useful knowledge, that he is one 'whom it is not worth while to take much trouble to accommodate.'"

But it is convenient even for those to whom the principles and means of research are best known, to be able to ascertain, readily, what books, of those which they know to have been written upon the subjects of their investigation, are to be found in the particular libraries which they consult. This end may be attained in the following manner. In connection with the *catalogue* of each library, there should be an *index* of subjects. This index should also be alphabetical. Under each subject, the divisions which naturally belong to it, should be distinctly recognized. It may here be remarked, that the parts of any particular science, or branch of learning, may be clearly defined, and universally acknowledged, whilst the relation of this science, or branch of learning, to others, may not be clearly established. To use the words of a vigorous writer upon this subject: "Take a library upon one science, and it classifies beautifully, sketching out, to a nicety, the boundaries, which, it is too rarely noticed, are much more distinct between the parts of a subject, than between one subject and another. Long after the counties of England and Scotland were well determined, the debateable land was nothing but a theatre of war."

This index should be alphabetical, rather than classed, because it is easier to find a word, in an alphabetical arrangement, than in any other order of classification; and, besides, the subject of research may be one not admitted, as a distinct division, in any classification. Such indexes can hardly be expected, immediately, in connection with the general catalogue; though, it is to be hoped, that these valuable appendages will not long be, of necessity, omitted.

A method of securing uniformity in such indexes may, hereafter, be agreed upon, so that they may be combined and form an alphabetical index of subjects to the general catalogue. It is thought best, however, for the present, to limit our efforts to the procuring of good alphabetical catalogues, as a groundwork, to which other valuable aids to research, may, as opportunities offer, be superadded.

## NECESSITY OF RULES FOR THE PREPARATION OF CATALOGUES.

The preparation of a catalogue may seem a light task, to the inexperienced, and to those who are unacquainted with the requirements of the learned world, respecting such works. In truth, however, there is no species of literary labor so arduous and perplexing. The peculiarities of titles are, like the idiosyncracies of authors, innumerable. Books are in all languages, and treat of subjects as multitudinous as the topics of human thought.

Liability to error and to confusion is, here, so great and so continual, that it is impossible to labor successfully, without a rigid adherence to rules. Although such rules be not formally enunciated, they must exist in the mind of the cataloguer, and guide him, or the result of his labors will be mortifying and unprofitable.

In this country, he who undertakes to prepare a catalogue, goes to the work under great disadvantages, in many respects. Few have had opportunity to acquire the requisite bibliographical knowledge and experience; and few libraries contain the necessary books of reference. A set of rules, therefore, seems peculiarly necessary for the assistance of librarians.

Minute and stringent rules become absolutely indispensable, when the catalogue of each library is, as upon the proposed plan, to form part of a general catalogue. *Uniformity* is, then, imperative; but, among many laborers, can only be secured by the adherence of all to rules embracing, as far as possible, the minutest details of the work.

The rules which follow were drawn up with great care. They are founded upon those adopted for the compilation of the catalogue of the British Museum; some of them are, *verbatim*, the same. Others conform more to rules advocated by Mr. Panizzi, than to those finally sanctioned by the Trustees of the Museum. Many modifications and additions have been made, adapted to the peculiar character of the system now proposed. Some innovations have been introduced, which, it is hoped, may be considered improvements. The commissioners, appointed to examine and report upon the catalogue project, considered not only its general features, but, also, its minute details. To them, were submitted the rules for cataloguing, which were separately discussed, and, after having been variously amended and modified, were recommended for adoption.

It is too much to suppose that any code should provide for every case of difficulty which may occur. The great aim, here, has been to establish principles, and to furnish analogies, by which many cases, not immediately discussed, may be indirectly settled; and, it is believed, that the instances will be few, which cannot be determined, by studying the rules, with the remarks under them, and carefully considering the characteristics of this kind of catalogue.

It should be remembered that a principal object of the rules is to secure *uniformity;* and that, consequently, some rules, which may seem unnecessarily burdensome, and, in certain applications, even capricious, are, all things considered, the best; because they secure that uniformity, which is not otherwise possible of attainment, and without which, the catalogues could not be comprehended in a general system.

## DUTIES OF COLLABORATORS AND SUPERINTENDENT.

The catalogue of each library is to be prepared, in accordance with the rules, under the immediate direction of the librarian, by transcribers employed by him. Should the system here proposed come into general use, it will probably be found expedient to have persons specially trained to the business, who shall go from place to place, for the purpose of making catalogues. Much of the value of the work will, of course, depend upon the faithfulness and learning of those who first prepare the titles. The qualifications, both natural and acquired, demanded for the suitable accomplishment of their task, are, unfortunately, rare. No person, who is impatient, indolent, inaccurate, or careless in his personal habits; who is ignorant of literary history and bibliography; who is unacquainted with the classical, and with the most important modern languages; or who is destitute of that general knowledge of the circle of the sciences, which is attained in, what is usually called, a liberal education; can be expected to make a catalogue of a general library, that will not be discreditable to the compiler, and to the institution employing him. Great care should, therefore, be exercised in selecting men for such work.

It is proper to remark, in this place, that no one, whatever may be his talents, attainments and industry, can safely work with the rapidity, which the public, and committees (inexperienced in catalogue-making, however judicious and well-instructed in other matters) frequently require. It is impossible to say what would be a good average rate of performance, in cataloguing a library, without knowing exactly the kind of works it contains. The best and only satisfactory criterion is furnished by the rate of progress in the British Museum, the National Library of Paris, and other large libraries containing books of all kinds. A trial of many years has shown that men possessed of the best qualifications, long practised in the work, with every advantage of a systematic division of labor, of access to all necessary books of reference, and to persons who could help them in emergencies, provided with every mechanical facility and assistance to be desired, can prepare about forty or fifty titles a day.

The danger of working with too great rapidity, without rules, and without suitable bibliographical preparation, was most strikingly illustrated during the discussions of the British Museum Commission. The following account of the particular instance alluded to is extracted from an article in the Edinburgh Review for October, 1850:

"Mr. Payne Collier, the secretary of the Commission, undertook to show how the Museum catalogue *should* be made, without reference to any preceding one. Mr. Collier prepared, according to his own views, twenty-five titles, done in an hour, of books from his own library, and with which he was therefore previously well acquainted. They were handed to Mr. Panizzi, with the full consent of the writer, and an invitation of criticism. Mr. Payne Collier is known to our readers: but to 'excuse the tone of confidence' he assumed, he described himself, in handing over these slips, as having attained a certain reputation in letters and particularly in antiquarian literature. The description is as correct a one as could be looked for from Mr. Collier himself: and the Society of Antiquaries, the Shakspeare and Camden Societies, and the Royal Society of Literature could inform the public, if need were, that he did not overrate himself. Moreover, his confidence was proved and supported by the most explicit dealing: he willingly lent those of the books he had described which were not in the Museum library, and, after the criticism to which we are coming, he offered no plea of haste. On the contrary, when a contemporary journal, of opposite views to our own, called them, by way of extenuation, his 'hurried slips,' he wrote a public letter in correction of the designation, maintaining that they were 'not hurried in any sense of the word,' and adhering to the defence, presently to be noticed, which he had circulated among the Commissioners in a private pamphlet.

"Mr. Panizzi put these slips into the hands of Mr. Jones, his senior assistant, requesting him to report upon them. The report was as follows:

'These twenty-five titles contain almost every possible error which can be committed in cataloguing books, and are open to almost every possible objection which can be brought against concise titles. The faults may be classed as follows:—1st. Incorrect or insufficient description, calculated to mislead as to the nature or condition of the work specified. 2nd. Omission of the names of editors, whereby we lose a most necessary guide in selecting among different editions of the same work. 3rd. Omission of the Christian names of authors, causing great confusion between the works of different authors who have the same surname—a confusion increasing in proportion to the extent of the catalogue. 4th. Omission of the names of annotators. 5th. Omission of the names of translators. 6th. Omission of the number of the edition, thus rejecting a most important and direct evidence of the value of a work. 7th. Adopting the name of the editor as a heading, when the name of the author appears in the title-page. 8th. Adopting the name of the translator as a heading, when the name of the author appears on the title-page. 9th. Adopting as a heading the title or name of the author merely as it appears on the title-page—a practice which would distribute the works of the Bishop of London under the names Blomfield, Chester, and London; and those of Lord Ellesmere under Gowan, Egerton, and Ellesmere. 10th. Using English or some other language instead of the language of the title-page. 11th. Cataloguing anonymous works, or works published under initials, under the name of the supposed author. Where this practice is adopted, the books so catalogued can be found only by those who possess the same information as the cataloguer, and uniformity of system is impossible, unless the cataloguer know the author of every work published anonymously or under initials. 12th. Errors in grammar. 13th. Errors in description of the size of the book. We have here faults of thirteen different kinds in twenty-five titles, and the number of these faults amount to more than two in each title. A large proportion of them, moreover, is of such a nature that it would be impossible to detect them when the written title is separated from the book: for example, Mr. Collier has catalogued an edition of the Odyssey, with a Latin title, as though the title were in Greek. A mere perusal of Mr. Collier's title would not lead any person to suspect the existence of such a blunder. [I may say (says Mr. Panizzi), by way of parenthesis, that when I saw this Odyssey, printed at Oxford, with a Greek title, I sent everywhere to try to find it. I had one with a Latin title of the same year, and of the same size, but I could not be sure that it was the same. I sent to Oxford; I made all sorts of inquiries; nobody knew such an Odyssey with a Greek title; but still this was negative evidence, until I begged the favor of Mr. Collier to show me the book itself from which he drew up his title. The title is in Latin, therefore the idea created by his title, that there was another edition of the Odyssey in the same year and of the same size, at Oxford, is wrong; there was only one.] Two editions of Madame de Stael's work on the French Revolution appeared at Paris in 1818: but Mr. Collier's title making no mention of the edition, the inference would arise that the copy to which it referred was of the *first* rather than of the *second* edition. It is a fallacy to say that errors can be corrected on a subsequent perusal of the titles or in print, unless that perusal be an actual comparison of the title with the book. [In fact, in the case of the Odyssey with the Greek title, the title looked to all intents and purposes very correct, but it was not correct.] Where we see such a result as is shown above, from an experiment made by a gentleman of education, accustomed to research, and acquainted with books generally, upon only twenty-five works, taken from his own library, and of the most easy description, we may form some idea of what a catalogue would be, drawn up, in the same manner, by ten persons, of about 600,000 works, embracing every branch of human learning, and presenting difficulties of every possible description. The average number of faults being more than two to a title, the total is somewhat startling—about 1,300,000 faults for the 600,000 works; that is, supposing the proportion to continue the same. But it must be borne in mind that the proportion of errors would increase with the number of titles; that to errors in drawing up each individual title would be superadded the errors which would unavoidably occur in the process of arranging the titles, and subsequently in the printing. In short, I humbly conceive that it would be impossible to prove the inexpediency of Mr. Collier's plan more effectually than he has himself done; and I hope I may add, without giving offence, that, had I seen these titles under any other circumstances than the present, I should have concluded that the object was to show how nearly worthless would be a catalogue, the proposed advantages of which were short titles, drawn up and printed within the shortest possible period of time.'

"Mr. Jones then proceeded to a detailed proof of his assertions. In a case of this kind, we are inclined to think that Mr. Collier should have had a reply: but the question is complicated, for though here assailed, he was an assailant, and moreover was an officer of the court who had been permitted to make himself a partizan, and to support his own views by circulating pamphlets among the judges, which a sense of official propriety prevented Mr. Panizzi from answering in the same way. Mr. Collier did answer in a pamphlet addressed to the Commissioners, as well as (recently) in the journal alluded to. The answer does not deny one iota of Mr. Jones's imputation: it merely protests against being tried by Mr. Panizzi's rules. 'I intended,' says Mr. Collier, 'my English mode of cataloguing to be diametrically opposed to his foreign mode, which might do well enough for stationary or retrograding countries, where want of enlightenment is at this hour producing the most lamentable

5

consequences, but which was totally unfit for this country, where inquiry is active, where education is daily extending, and which mainly owes to the spread of education* the happiness and tranquillity it enjoys. Nothing therefore could be more obviously unjust than *to test my titles by Mr. Panizzi's rules.* I discarded them altogether; I threw them overboard at once, and *en masse.* . . . . .'

"We are English as well as Mr. Collier; but we do not see that progress and enlightenment are essentially connected with bad bibliography at two errors and a fraction per title. Neither do we think Mr. Collier's defence more valid than would be that of an incorrect arithmetician who should attribute the rules to Cocker or Walkingame, and protest against the jurisdiction. Mr. Panizzi's rules, like all other codes, contain offences divisible into *mala in se* and *mala prohibita:* Mr. Collier justifies his departures from the morals of bibliography, by alleging his right to differ from Mr. Panizzi about its expediencies. He leaves out an author's Christian name, or substitutes his translator for him, and says he is not bound to follow Mr. Panizzi's foreign modes: and therein he resembles those reasoners who have defended false inference by renouncing Aristotle. But his own argument may be turned against him: it is a strong presumption in favor of the materiality of Mr. Panizzi's rules, that so able an opponent finds himself under the necessity of implying the following alternative—either those rules, or such bibliography as is seen in *this* rejection of them. We dwell the more upon this point because we observe that some of the journals adopt the defence, and say in terms that what Mr. Panizzi calls errors are deviations from his own ninety-one rules. Are we really to believe that, if Mr. Collier had chosen to spell authors' names backwards, it would have been a sufficient answer to an objection from Mr. Panizzi, that the plan of writing them forwards was one of his own rules? According to Mr. Collier and his defenders, *English grammar* is only one of Mr. Panizzi's foreign modes, repudiated by English common sense."

But the most elaborately formed rules for cataloguing are inadequate to provide for all cases. Doubts and difficulties will unavoidably arise, as to their application. For example, in abridging titles, scarcely any two men would agree, even within the limits of the rules given. It is necessary, therefore, that there should be a central superintendence of the whole enterprise; and that the duties of those who are engaged in preparing the titles, and of the superintendent should be distinctly understood. This object has been kept in view in preparing the rules. The transcribers are to be responsible for

* We understand Mr. Collier to imply that education is much more extended in England than in Prussia.

exactness, in writing off titles without abridgment; and for a clear statement, in notes, of all peculiarities not mentioned in the titles. They should also indicate the parts of the titles which they think might be omitted.

The titles are then to be submitted to the superintendent. He is to examine them, in order to see that all the rules have been observed. He is to decide upon all abridgments and additions, and mark the manuscript for the printer. He is also to examine the last revise.

## PRINTING AND STEREOTYPING.

The printing should all be executed in one office, under the immediate eye of the superintendent. The same type, and the same style of work should be used in all parts.

It is not necessary, upon this plan, to finish a catalogue in manuscript, before beginning to print. Titles may be prepared and stereotyped without regard to their future arrangement. The work of the printer may keep pace with that of the transcribers. Should it be desired, a catalogue might be published in parts, each comprising a particular class of books.

The titles, after having been set up in type, and corrected with the utmost care, are, before stereotyping, to be sent to the library to which they belong, to be revised, by a comparison with the books themselves. This arrangement implies the necessity of a large fount of type, and of promptness on the part of librarians.

The titles are then to be stereotyped, each upon a separate plate, or block. The headings (if they be names) are to stand on plates distinct from the titles. This is required, in order to avoid repeating them for each title. They must be separate from the titles, that other titles may, if occasion require, be interposed.

Every name, or other word, used as a heading, is to be printed, in the title, in small capitals; thus each stereotyped title will show, at a glance, the heading under which it belongs.

Each title is to have upon it a running number, according to the order of its being stereotyped. The use of this number is for reference to the *Local Index* of the general catalogue, in which the libraries, where the books are to be found, will be designated. When the catalogue is made up, these numbers will not be in connection; but in the index, they will follow each other in consecutive order, and should there have, printed against each, the names of the several libraries containing the book. These numbers will further serve to show the extent and progress of the work.

Copies of the titles stereotyped will be kept at the Smithsonian Institution, arranged in their numerical order; so that in referring to any particular title it may not be necessary to copy the title in full, but merely to give the number attached to it.

It will sometimes happen, that words, which, according to the rules, are used as headings, do not occur in the titles. There would, then, without further provision, be no means of ascertaining, from an examination of the plate itself, its order in the collection. To meet this case, the expedient has been adopted, of setting up the word to be used as the heading, in the margin of the title, and in shorter type, which will then show itself upon the plate, but not upon the printed page.

## PRESERVATION AND USE OF THE PLATES.

When the titles have been stereotyped, and the plates ascertained to be in perfect working order, they are to be arranged alphabetically, and kept on sliding shelves, or shallow drawers, placed as near to each other as possible. The catch-letters of the titles may be marked upon the front of each shelf, so as to admit of alteration as the changing of the plates may require. The ranges of shelves may be so disposed as to form deep and narrow alcoves. A room of fifty feet by forty would accommodate the plates of upwards of a million titles, which may, in this manner, be kept in very compact and perfect order, and, at the same time, be easily accessible.

It may not be amiss to add, that the material, which it is proposed to employ in the stereotyping, is much less expensive than common type metal; so cheap, indeed, that the whole expenditure on this account, even for so large a collection, would be of small importance. It is, besides, much lighter than type metal, more convenient in handling, and requires fewer, and less expensive fixtures. It is not at all affected by dampness, or by any ordinary elevation of temperature.

The plates are mounted, for printing, upon blocks similar to those ordinarily used for stereotype plates, but with continuous clamps extending the whole length of the page. The breadth of page adopted is such as is suitable for a work in octavo, or in double columns in quarto or folio. The latter form (folio double columns) will probably be found most convenient, as well as most economical, for large catalogues. Presenting more titles upon a page, it enables a student to examine and compare, with greater facility, the various works of an author. It requires also less paper and press-work for the same number of titles. These considerations have led to the general adoption of the folio form for catalogues of large libraries. To these it may be added, in the present case, that in folio pages it would be practicable to avoid the division of titles between lines, without occasioning observable irregularities in the length of the pages.

## METHOD OF USING THE STEREOTYPED TITLES IN THE FORMATION OF NEW CATALOGUES.

In concluding these details of the system of stereotyping catalogues, by separate titles, it now remains to say a few words upon the method of employing the titles, in the construction of new catalogues.

Whenever, after the publication of one catalogue, upon this plan, it should be proposed to form a catalogue of another library, the first step would be to ascertain, which of the titles of such library have been already stereotyped; for these need not again be transcribed.

This may be done in the following manner. A copy of the catalogue already published, together with a copy of any titles which may have been subsequently stereotyped, should be sent to the cataloguer, who as he takes a book from the shelf should first seek for its title among those already printed. If a title, strictly identical with that of the book, be found, it should be marked in the margin.

When titles occur, which he does not find among those already printed, they are to be written, each on a card or slip of paper, according to the rules; and, as the work goes on, sent, in parcels, to be stereotyped.

When the cataloguer has gone through the library in this manner, he is to return the printed catalogues, in the margin of which he has marked the common titles. The printer will then be able to select and combine the plates to be used for this particular catalogue, impose them, print the requisite number of copies, and distribute them to their places.

After the catalogues of several libraries shall have been thus prepared and printed, they will be combined to form a general catalogue of those libraries, and thus the labor of selecting common titles will always be limited within narrow bounds.

# RULES.

# RULES FOR PREPARING CATALOGUES.

## TITLES.

I. The Titles are to be transcribed IN FULL, including the names of Authors, Editors, Translators, Commentators, Continuators, &c., precisely as they stand upon the title-page.

EXCEPTIONS. There are many titles from which much may well be omitted. But to make omissions without prejudice to ready investigation is an extremely difficult and delicate task, in the performance of which, uniformity is highly important; it is therefore desirable that all abridgments be made by the same person. To this end, the rule should stand without exception, so far as the writing out of the titles is concerned. The abridgments for printing should all be made by the superintendent, and only in the following cases:

Additions to names of authors, &c., not necessary for their identification; mottoes, repetitions, or expletives not essential to a full and clear titular description of the book, may be omitted. Omissions of mottoes and devices are to be denoted by three stars; of other matter, by three dots, placed thus . . .

No omission is to be made which requires any change in, or addition to, the phraseology of that part of the title which is retained. Not even an improvement of the title, by any change, is to be allowed.

REMARK 1. This rule is understood to apply only to the principal entry. It is supposed that each title will be entered in full only once. All other entries will refer to this full entry. They will be called *Cross-References;* and rules for their preparation are given hereafter.

Remark 2. It is necessary (in this plan) to give the name of the Author, in connection with the title, although it be but a repetition of the heading; for the heading will be stereotyped separate from the title, and, therefore, the title should contain all that is necessary to indicate its proper position, in the alphabetical order, in case of displacement.

Remark 3. Experience shows that it takes less time to transcribe titles in full, than to abridge them with any tolerable degree of accuracy. It requires, too, less learning and experience in the cataloguer. That a catalogue can be made more rapidly, more economically, and more satisfactorily by transcribing the titles faithfully and fully, without the omission of a single letter or point, than by any proper plan of abridgment, cannot be denied by any one who has fairly tried the experiment.* If the catalogue were not to be printed, this rule should have no exception whatever. The printing, however, introduces two considerations to modify the rule, namely, the *expense* of printing, and the *bulk* of the catalogue. The force of the former consideration is much diminished by the plan of stereotyping the titles. It is but a first expense that we have to meet, not a repetition of it. Besides, no library but the first has to print all its titles. The saving, even to the second library, by the use of those already stereotyped, would doubtless far more than counterbalance the extra expense of printing long titles. The bulk of the catalogue is certainly a matter of considerable importance, though of less than might, at first, be supposed. It does not make much difference, in convenience of use, whether such a work as an Encyclopædia be in a hundred volumes or in ten, though it is, of course, more convenient to refer to one volume than to ten. The proposed general catalogue would doubtless exceed one volume, even with short titles. But convenience should not be allowed to have more influence than the demands of learned investigators. The bulk of catalogues should not be considered in opposition to their accuracy, and to such a degree

*A very complete discussion of the comparative advantages of long and short titles is contained in the Report of the Commissioners on the British Museum, with Minutes of Evidence, 1850, particularly in Mr. Panizzi's Letter to the Earl of Ellesmere, in Appendix No. 12.

of fulness of title, as may be necessary to identify the book, and to give all such particulars of information, as may justly be expected from a titular description.

REMARK 4. It is deemed unnecessary to prescribe any particular form of card or paper for use in copying the titles. If they are to be printed at once, it will be found most convenient to write them on one side only of common foolscap paper. Cross references should immediately follow the titles to which they belong. If cards have already been adopted in the library to be catalogued, their form need not be changed. They may be placed in the hands of the printer without being transcribed. A manuscript catalogue for constant use should generally be upon cards. A very convenient method of keeping them is that employed by Mr. Folsom in the Boston Athenæum. The cards are long and narrow; are so perforated that they may be strung upon cords, which, being elastic, allow free motion without displacement; and are kept in cases, made to resemble folio volumes, one side of which opens like the cover of a book.

## II. The Titles are to be transcribed WITH EXACTNESS.

REMARK 1. The titles are *not to be translated* by the cataloguer. If, however, the original title, being in a language which does not admit of being represented in the Roman character, be accompanied by a translation into a language for which the Roman alphabet may be used, the latter may be given without the former; this peculiarity being mentioned, with such explanations as will prevent mistake as to the language in which the book is printed. If the book be in several languages, and be provided with title-pages for each, or for several, the cataloguer may give the preference to languages using the Roman alphabet in the following order: English, Latin, French, Italian, Spanish, German. The other title-pages should however be mentioned.

REMARK 2. The *precise phraseology*, however quaint, awkward, or ungrammatical, must be scrupulously followed. When striking faults or errors occur, the cataloguer should write [*sic*], after each of them, to denote that the title has been faithfully copied, and that the error is not attributable to his carelessness.

REMARK 3. The exact mode of *spelling*, however inaccurate or antiquated, must be conscientiously copied. When abbreviations appear upon the title-page, they should, in transcribing, be copied accurately. They should also, if possible, be printed. These are most frequent in early printed Latin and Greek books. If types cannot be had for printing these abbreviations, the word should be given in full; the added letters being italics.

REMARK 4. The *punctuation* of the title-page should also be retained. Sometimes, in the titles of modern books, no pointing is used; in such cases, none should be introduced. Wide spaces may be used instead.

REMARK 5. The *accentuation* of the original should be preserved. In French books, however, it often happens that parts of the title-page are printed in capitals without accents, and other parts in "lower-case" letters with accents. This is attributable to the general want of accents upon what are called "title-letters." To avoid the striking incongruity which would be occasioned by printing one part with, and another without accents, when the same letter is used throughout the title. it will be proper to add the accents, where they are omitted in the titles of foreign books; but not to omit or alter any which occur.

REMARK 6. When possible, the *form of letter* (as Black Letter, Italic, Greek, Hebrew, &c.), is to be preserved. When Black Letter, Italic, or any peculiar letter or cut of type is used, in the title, merely as a typographical embellishment, it is not to be copied; but only when the whole book is printed in it. This rule has no limitation, except the knowledge of the cataloguer, and the means of the printing office. With reference to those languages in which is embodied the great mass of literature, there will be little difficulty in finding men to copy the titles with accuracy; and the printing office should contain varieties of type, Roman, Black Letter, German, Greek, Hebrew, and, in time, fonts of other alphabets.

Books in languages which cannot, at first, be correctly printed or written, should be reported from each library, as accurately and fully as possible. An arrangement may hereafter be made to employ competent persons to catalogue such works, and means may be procured for printing or engraving their titles. No title, however, should be stereotyped for the General Catalogue, till its accuracy and conformity to the rules are fully ascertained.

REMARK 7. This principle does not apply to the *use of capitals or small letters*. Most title-pages are printed wholly in large letters; some are partly in large and partly in small letters. For the catalogue, they are to be written and printed in small letters.

REMARK 8. *Initial capitals* are to be used only when the laws of the language now require them. In English, the first word of every sentence, proper names, adjectives derived from proper names, names of the Deity, the first word of the title of a book quoted within another title, and titles of respect or office, such as Hon., Mr., Dr., Capt., Rev., (whether contracted or not,) prefixed to a name, should be written and printed with initial capitals. In German and Danish, every noun begins with a capital. In French, Spanish, Italian and Portuguese, adjectives derived from proper names, are not, as in English, generally printed with initial capitals. In Latin, the English usage in this particular should be followed. It would doubtless be more satisfactory to make the titles, as printed in the catalogue, perfect transcripts of the title-pages, in respect to the use of initial capitals; but this is hardly practicable. The use of both upper-case and lower-case letters in a title-page, is for the most part a matter of the printer's taste, and does not generally indicate the author's purpose. To copy them in a catalogue with literal exactness would be exceedingly difficult, and of no practical benefit. In those parts of the title-page which are printed wholly in capitals, initials are undistinguished. It would be unsightly and un-undesirable to distinguish the initials where the printer had done so, and omit them where he had used a form of letter, which prohibited his distinguishing them. It would teach nothing to copy from the book the initial capitals in one part of the title, and allow the cataloguer to supply them in other parts. The only practicable method of securing uniformity or convenience would seem to be, to require, as is done above, the cataloguer to employ initial capitals according to established laws, regardless of the title-page.

There are certain features of title-pages which it is wholly impracticable to transfer to a catalogue. For example, they generally are (as they always should be) *inscriptions*, and as such are meant to have a certain *local disposition* of parts which serves to interpret them, by showing at a glance their relations to each other. A title in a catalogue cannot be expected to retain this important feature of an inscription.

III. The whole Title is to be repeated for every distinct edition of the work; and the number of the edition, if not the first, is to be always given.

REMARK 1. The necessity of this rule arises from the stereotyping of the titles separately. It is frequently the case, that publishers, after having stereotyped a book, call every thousand copies of it a separate edition, and, for twenty or more editions, there may be no alteration in the book, except in the word expressing the number of the edition, and in the date. In such cases, it cannot be necessary to print a separate title for each pretended edition. If there be any important alteration of the book, it should be designated as a distinct edition. This irregularity is found mostly, if not exclusively, in American books, and occurs principally in school-books.

It is easy to see how this artifice of bibliopoles would occasion great trouble to cataloguers, if it were common. Some publishers have introduced the terms "second thousand," "tenth thousand," &c., instead of "second edition," "tenth edition." This is more honest, and for our purposes more convenient. But it is not necessary to introduce these chiliads into the catalogue.

Minor changes are sometimes made in the stereotype plates, after a part of the copies have been printed; that is, some error may be discovered and corrected, or some word substituted for another. But such changes are generally slight and unimportant. They can only be detected by comparing one copy of a book with another, and, when known, are seldom worthy of notice.

Sometimes, the title of a book is the same in two editions, while the body of the work is more or less altered. Sometimes, also, the title is changed while the book remains entirely unaltered. Such instances are, however, of comparatively rare occurrence. They are, or should be, noted in bibliographical dictionaries. It is not often the case, that the two editions are to be found in one library; consequently, an account of such variations cannot be expected from the cataloguer. But, if such facts become known to him, they should be carefully noted.

The increase of the bulk of the catalogue, which this rule will occasion, may appear, at first sight, to be a grave difficulty. It should be considered, however, that the number of books, which reach a second edition, is comparatively small; and, that, although there may be a hundred editions of a book, those only will have their titles repeated, which belong to the library to be catalogued. The increase in bulk will be much less considerable than might be apprehended, and it will be more than compensated for, by the greater exactness of the descriptions. Any one, who has had much experience in examining catalogues, must have been frequently puzzled to ascertain the exact character of several editions of a book, where the only description of any edition after the first, is "*The same*," or "*Ditto*," with a different date. We may wish to know whether the titles are identical. In the title of a later edition, some particular may have been given, which to us is very important, but which the cataloguer has omitted. To bibliographers, and men of habits of careful investigation, different editions are different books, and they should be always described, in catalogues, as particularly as if they were independent works.

IV. Early printed books, without title-pages, are to be catalogued in the words of the head-title, preceded by the word [*Beginning*], in italics and between brackets; to which are to be added the words of the colophon, preceded by the word [*Ending*], in italics and between brackets.

If there be neither head-title nor colophon, such a description of the work should be given, in English, and between brackets, as may serve for its identification.

REMARK 1. Books printed before the adoption of separate title-pages are comparatively few. Most of them have been described with great minuteness by bibliographers, particularly by Maittaire, Denis, Panzer, and Hain. It will be best, in all cases, to refer to their works in cataloguing such books.

These books generally have at the beginning a head-title, which contains a sufficient description of the book, while in the colophon the place of publication, name of the printer, date, &c., are given; but sometimes the book begins with a table, or dedication, or register, and has no colophon. In such cases, not unfrequently, there is a title at the end of the table, or in the dedication. In short, so great is the variety of cases, that it would be extremely difficult, if not impossible, to give rules applicable to them all. The rule given above will, it is thought, be found sufficiently comprehensive.

V. In cataloguing Academical Dissertations, Orations, &c., the subject-matter is to be given as the title. If that be not expressed upon the title-page, it is to be supplied within brackets, if possible in the words of the author, otherwise in English and in italics. The contracted words [*Diss. Ac.*] when necessary to indicate the character of the publication, should be prefixed. The occasion may generally be omitted, except when the subject of the dissertation or oration has some special reference to it.

VI. In cataloguing Sermons, the book, chapter and verse of the *text;* the *date*, if it differs from that of publication; and the *occasion*, if a special one, are to be given. When these are not upon the title-page, they are to be supplied between brackets, and in italics.

VII. Periodical publications are to be recorded in the

words of the title-page of the last complete volume; but without designation of volume or date.

The history of the publication from its commencement, including all changes of form, title, editorship, &c., is to be given in a note.

REMARK 1. This rule applies to Reviews, Magazines, &c.; not to works issued in parts, sometimes called "serials," nor to transactions of learned societies.

REMARK 2. The last title is preferred for the catalogue, because it is that by which the work is currently known, and because of the peculiar difficulty of finding complete sets of these publications. If the title be changed, it will become necessary to prepare a new one for the catalogue, and to make an addition to the note.

VIII. After the words of the title, the number of parts, volumes, fasciculi, or whatever may be the peculiar divisions of each work, is to be specified.

When nothing is said, in the title, respecting this point, if the work be divided into several portions, but the same paging continue, or, when the pages are not numbered, if the same register continue, the work is to be considered as divided into *parts* (not volumes). If the progressive number of the pages, or the register be interrupted, then each series of pages, or of letters of the register, is to be designated as a *volume.*

REMARK 1. In designating volumes when the number is not stated upon the title-page, the words Volume, Tome, Theil, Band, Deel, &c., may generally be represented by the initials alone. The numbers may be always expressed by Arabic figures. If the ordinal expression of number be used on the title-page, the figures may be given, and the ordinal termination omitted. The numbers of the first and of the last volume only are to be given, with a dash between them, thus:

| | | |
|---|---|---|
| V. 1—8. | for | Volume 1—Volume 8, i.e. Volume first—Volume eighth, or First Volume—Eighth Volume. |
| B. 2—22. | " | Zweiter Band—Zwei und zwanzigster Band. |
| T. 1—4. | " | Tomo 1—Tomo 4. |
| Th. 1—6. | " | Theil 1—Theil 6. |

REMARK 2. When there is a discrepancy between the number of divisions of a work indicated on the title-page, and the actual number of volumes, as defined above, (that is, of divisions with separate pagings), the number of *pagings* should be stated;—each paging being considered a distinct volume. The paging of the preface and introductory matter is to be excepted. Appendixes, when separately paged, should be specially noticed in the title, though not reckoned as separate volumes.

IX. Next should follow the designation of the PLACE and DATE of publication. The name of the place should be given in the form and language of the title-page. If, in that, it be abbreviated, the full name should be supplied, but not translated; the added parts being between brackets.

Should either of these particulars be omitted in the title-page, the deficiency should be supplied from the knowledge of the librarian, or be noticed, in italics and between brackets.

REMARK 1. It would on many accounts be desirable to give the name of the publisher, but, as it would add very much to the labor of preparation, and considerably increase the size of the catalogue, it is thought best not to do so.

REMARK 2. In the case of early printed books, and typographical rarities, or where several editions of the same book are known to have been published in the same year and place, by different publishers, the name of the publisher should be specified.

REMARK 3. The date is to be given in Arabic figures, unless numerals be used in the title-page, in such a manner as to be on some accounts distinctive.

X. Next after the imprint should follow the designation of SIZE.

In accordance with general usage, the fold of the sheet, as folio, quarto, octavo, when it can be ascertained, is to be stated. As an additional, and more exact designation of size, the *Height and Breadth of the first full signature page* (the folio and signature lines being omitted in the measurement) are to be stated in inches and tenths, the fractions being expressed decimally.

EXPLANATION 1. The librarian should use a small square or rule, marked with inches and tenths. The first number given should represent the height, and the second, the breadth of the page. In the catalogue, the measurement would be recorded thus:—

8° (7.3×4.2)

that is, fold of sheet, 8vo; measuring, 7 inches and 3 tenths in height, by 4 inches and 2 tenths in breadth.

EXPLANATION 2. When the first signature page is not a full page, or when it has foot notes, turn to the first succeeding signature page which is full and without notes.

EXPLANATION 3. When there are no signatures, measure the first full *recto* page. If the other pages vary much from the standard page, add *irr.* for *irregular.*

EXPLANATION 4. Marginal rules and side marginal references and notes are not to be regarded in the measurement; some editions may be printed with and some without them. But such marginal references should be mentioned.

EXPLANATION 5. Catch-words generally stand upon the signature line, and are therefore not to be counted. The measurement of height should, however, comprise all printed matter below the folio line, and above the signature line. By folio line is meant that upon which stands the number of the page.

REMARKS. The designation of the form is added to the titles of books in catalogues for two purposes: to enable one to distinguish between different editions of the same book, and to convey to those who have not seen the book, some idea of its size.

The fold of the paper has been universally adopted, as the measure of size. A sheet once folded, forming two leaves, or four pages, is a folio. A sheet twice folded, forming four leaves or eight pages, is a quarto. A sheet three times folded, forming eight leaves, or sixteen pages, is an octavo. A sheet so folded as to form twelve leaves, or twenty-four pages, is a duodecimo. And so on.

But this method of designating the size of a book is inexact and frequently deceptive; because, 1st, it is not always possible to ascertain the fold; and, 2dly, the fold, when ascertained, gives no definite indication of the size or shape of the book.

In many books one can tell, at a glance, the fold of the sheet; but it is unsafe to rely upon this first impression. Examination of signatures is indispensable. Sometimes, it is necessary to examine also the water-lines and water-marks. Occasionally, all these will fail us.

*Signatures* are letters or figures placed at the bottom of the first page of each sheet, as guides to the binder, to denote the order of the sheets. The signatures of the different forms from folio to 32mo, would regularly be placed as follows:

| | | | | | | | | | |
|---|---|---|---|---|---|---|---|---|---|
| Folio, sheet, | on pages | 1, | 5, | 9, | 13, | 17, | 21, | &c. |
| Quarto, " | " | " | 1, | 9, | 17, | 25, | 33, | 41, | &c. |
| Octavo, " | " | " | 1, | 17, | 33, | 49, | 65, | 81, | &c. |
| 8vo, ½ sheet, | " | " | 1, | 9, | 17, | 25, | 33, | 41, | &c. |
| 12mo, sheet, | " | " | 1, | 25, | 49, | 73, | 97, | 121, | &c. |
| 12mo, ½ sheet, | " | " | 1, | 13, | 25, | 37, | 49, | 61, | &c. |
| 16mo, sheet, | " | " | 1, | 33, | 65, | 97, | 129, | 161, | &c. |
| 16mo, ½ sheet, | " | " | 1, | 17, | 33, | 49, | 65, | 81, | &c. |
| 18mo, sheet, | " | " | 1, | 37, | 73, | 109, | 145, | 181, | &c. |
| 18mo, ½ sheet, | " | " | 1, | 19, | 37, | 55, | 73, | 91, | &c. |
| 24mo, sheet, | " | " | 1, | 49, | 97, | 145, | 193, | 241, | &c. |

| | | | | | | | | | |
|---|---|---|---|---|---|---|---|---|---|
| 24mo, ½ sheet, | " | " | 1, | 25, | 49, | 73, | 97, | 121, | &c. |
| 32mo, sheet, | " | " | 1, | 65, | 129, | 193, | 257, | 321, | &c. |
| 32mo, ½ sheet, | " | " | 1, | 33, | 65, | 97, | 129, | 161, | &c. |

But sometimes the paging of the book begins in the midst of a signature; in such cases the signatures would fall on pages different from the above, throughout the book, though the intervals would be regular. Double signatures are sometimes placed upon stereotype plates, to enable printers to impose them either as octavos or duodecimos.

Besides the principal signatures, there are subordinate signatures, which, as they do not help to distinguish the size of the book, but are only used to aid the binder, are omitted in the above table.

It will be seen from this table, that the signatures are precisely the same for 8vos, in half sheets, as for 4tos; for 16mos, in half sheets, as for 8vos; for 24mos, in half sheets, as for 12mos; for 32mos, in half sheets, as for 16mos.

Printers impose in half sheets or sheets, according to their convenience. Of course, therefore, from the signatures *alone*, it is impossible to distinguish between 4tos and 8vos, 8vos and 16mos, 12mos and 24mos, 16mos and 32mos. It is generally easy to determine the fold by the size and shape of the book, but (as we shall show hereafter) not *always*.

Signatures do not occur in the earliest printed books; but as this class of books is small, and very particularly described by Panzer, Hain, and others, there is but little difficulty in ascertaining the precise description of them.

Books may be quired in printing, that is, several sheets may be put together, like the sheets in a quire of paper. In this case the principal signature is the same as if the whole formed only one sheet. A folio may thus be undistinguishable from an 8vo, by the signatures alone.

When signatures fail us, resort may sometimes be had to the water lines, which, by holding the paper up to the light, may be seen crossing the sheet perpendicularly, in the folio, 8vo, 18mo, 24mo, and 32mo; and horizontally, in all the other forms less than 32mo; sometimes, also, in the 24mo. The water-mark is a device of the manufacturer, placed in the middle of the half sheet, and distinguishable in the same way as the water-line. In the folio, this occurs in the middle of the page; in the quarto, in the back or fold of the book; in the 8vo, at the upper and inner corner. At the present day, however, printing paper is seldom made with water-lines or water-marks.

In examining a book, all these means of determining its fold occasionally deceive the most skilful bibliographer. If sheets of paper had, from the first, been always made of the same size, there would be comparatively little difficulty. But they have always varied so much, that a very small 8vo is often in no way distinguishable, in dimensions, from a large 16mo. Many other sizes also are liable to be confounded.

The following measurements, in inches, of a leaf of folio, octavo, and 16mo, of foolscap, medium, and imperial paper, will show how impossible it would be, from the size of the book to determine the fold of the sheet, even of paper of what are called the regular sizes, particularly when the books have been cut down in binding:

| | Folio, | Octavo, | 16mo. |
|---|---|---|---|
| Foolscap, | $13\frac{3}{4} \times 8\frac{3}{8}$, | $6\frac{5}{8} \times 4\frac{1}{4}$, | $4\frac{1}{4} \times 3\frac{3}{8}$, |
| Medium, | $18\frac{1}{4} \times 11\frac{1}{2}$, | $9\frac{1}{8} \times 5\frac{3}{4}$, | $5\frac{3}{4} \times 4\frac{1}{2}$, |
| Imperial, | $21\frac{7}{8} \times 15$, | $11 \times 7\frac{1}{2}$, | $7\frac{1}{2} \times 5\frac{1}{2}$, |

Since the introduction of machine paper and large presses, paper is made of almost any and every size and shape, and it is no longer possible to distinguish, with accuracy, the different folds. Books, which, judged by the eye, would be supposed to be quartos, are, in reality, duodecimos; books which might be supposed to be octavos, are 16mos, &c. The signatures, as we have seen, will not inform us whether a book is an 8vo, or a 16mo on half sheets. There are no water-marks to help us; nor is it possible in any way to tell.

If it be thus difficult, and often impossible, to ascertain the fold with the book before us, of what use can it be, as a designation of size, to those who have only the description? This is a difficulty which has but commenced. It is becoming more serious every year. It is more serious in America, than in other countries, for in Europe, there is much more regularity in the sizes of paper than here.

On these accounts, it has been thought desirable, if not indispensable, to introduce some new method of designating the size of books. The measurement of the printed page has seemed the readiest and most useful. The trouble of measuring is much less than might, at first sight, be supposed, and the time occupied by it is hardly worthy of consideration.

It would be, for all purposes of bibliography, better to make this the universal method of designating the size of books. It would save numberless blunders and frequent perplexity; and, upon the whole, would take less of the librarian's time, than the ordinary process of ascertaining the fold, provided that be done with exactness.

XI. In books of one volume, the body of which does not contain more than one hundred pages, the number of pages is to be specified. In applying this rule, copy the number of the last page of the body of the book, or of any addition paged continuously with it.

Remark 1. The value of catalogues would, doubtless, be enhanced by giving the number of pages in every volume, after the manner of Dryander in the Catalogue of Sir Joseph Banks's library; or with even greater particularity, thus: *pp. xxvi*+345+xlv, meaning 26 pages of prefatory matter, 345 pages in the body of the book, and 45 pages of appendix. But the disproportionate amount of additional labor, as well as of increase in the bulk and cost of catalogues, which such enumeration and notation would demand, renders it necessary to limit the object of this rule, which is to show whether the work described be merely of pamphlet size.

Remark 2. Prefatory matter is not to be included in the enumeration of pages. But if it be something more than a preface or introduction by the author, and deemed of sufficient importance to be added to the title, the number of pages of such prefatory matter should be included in the addition.

XII. All additions to the titles are to be printed in italics, and between brackets; to be in the English language, whatever be the language of the title; to be such only as are applicable to all copies of the edition described, and necessary for a full titular description of the book.

EXCEPTION. When parts of a name are supplied within brackets, they are to be in the vernacular of the author, whatever be the language of the title; and, if the name be used for the heading, the part supplied in the title is to correspond in typography with the rest of the name; that is, to be printed in small capitals.

REMARK 1. It is not always easy to say what additions are necessary, to render a title satisfactorily descriptive. A title is often a mere name, arbitrarily chosen by the author. It is sometimes allegorical, or embodies, in a pun, or conceit, or covert allusion, some indication of the subject-matter of the book. In such cases, it was not designed to be descriptive of the work, and could not be made so, without destroying its character. Explanations of such titles may be thought desirable; but if so, they should be given in notes, and separate from the titles themselves. A title should be the briefest possible designation of the contents of a book. It should cover everything which the book contains, but in the most general terms, without minute specifications. Mindful of this definition, we shall frequently find cases, where the title, intended to be descriptive, fails to give us what we have a right to expect. A book may be in a different language from the title-page. It may be in several languages, while the title indicates but one. It may contain an important Preface, Introduction, or Biography of the author, by another hand, not mentioned in the title. In these, and in many other cases, additions to the titles may be necessary.

REMARK 2. There are many cases, however, where it seems desirable to give further information concerning a work, than could be given within the title, under the restrictions of the preceding paragraph. The title may be a misnomer, or it may contain allusions, which it is desirable to explain. The book may be a rare and valuable one, with maps and illustrations, the number and description of which ought to be given. It may have been privately printed, or limited to a small number of copies, or prohibited, or condemned to be burnt. The edition may be the *Editio princeps*, or a fac-simile of an early edition, or a surreptitious or spurious edition; or it may be identical, except in the title, with what purports to be another edition, or an independent work. These facts belong, more properly, to a bibliographical dictionary, than to a catalogue. It is proper, however, that they should be noted by cataloguers. They may, also, be printed, at the discretion of the superintendent, but generally, in the form of separate notes, rather than as additions to the titles.

REMARK 3. Peculiarities of copies, such as large paper, satin paper, vellum; also notes, autographs, cancelled leaves, substituted leaves, mutilations and alterations; binding in a different number of volumes from that indicated in the title, or ascertained by the rule already given, &c. &c.,—these, and other peculiarities or imperfections of copy, relate only to particular copies, and therefore should not be noticed in a title intended to apply to the whole edition. Every cataloguer should, however, note every such thing, after the title. The note may be printed in the catalogue of the library containing the book described, but not, usually, in the title for the General Catalogue.

---

## HEADINGS.

XIII. When the title has been transcribed in accordance with the foregoing rules, the heading is to be written above it.

This heading determines the place of the title in the alphabetical catalogue, and consists, in general, of the name of the author in its vernacular form, when the same can be represented by the letters of the English alphabet.

When the word cannot be exactly represented by English letters, the form used by the best English authorities is to be adopted.

The surname is to be printed in capitals. Christian or first names are to follow, if possible in full, printed in small capitals, and within parentheses.

XIV. When a name is variously spelled, the best authorized orthography is to be selected for the heading, and such other modes of spelling the name, as are likely to occasion difficulty, are to be added, within brackets.

Cross references are to be made from all other forms of the name, which occur in the catalogue, to the form preferred.

XV. The following rules are to be observed in cataloguing names with prefixes:

(1.) If the name has become an English surname, it is to be recorded under the prefix, which is to be accounted as a part of the name.

Thus: *D'Israeli*, *De Morgan*, *De la Beche*, *Du Ponceau* are to be placed under *D*; *Van Buren* under *V*.

In such cases, cross-references are to be made from the principal name.

Names beginning with *Mac*, *O'*, *Ap*, and *Fitz*, are to be recorded under those syllables.

*Mc*, and *M'*, abbreviated forms of *Mac*, are to be considered the same as if written in full.

(2.) French surnames preceded by the preposition *de* are to be catalogued under the name itself, and not under the prefix.

Thus: *Florian (Jean Pierre Claris de)* is to be placed under *F*, not under *D*; *Alembert (Jean le Rond d')* under *A*, not under *D*.

In this respect, usage is by no means uniform among French authors. Thus, Brunet places *D'Alembert* under *D*, while Quérard, the Editors of the "Biographie Universelle," etc., place the same name under *A*. But consistency is of the first importance, and it is decidedly best to make this rule positive, and without exceptions.

(3.) French surnames preceded by *De la*, are to be recorded under the article.

Thus: *La Pérouse (Jean François Galaup de)*, not *De la Pérouse*, nor *Pérouse*; *La Harpe (Jean François de)*, not *De la Harpe*, nor *Harpe*.

It is better to make this the invariable rule, although uniformity will not be found among French writers, in this particular, nor scarcely consistency in any one writer.

(4.) French names preceded by *Du* or *Des* are to be recorded under these prefixes.

Thus: *Du Halde*, under *D*, not under *H*; *Des Cartes*, under *D*, not under *C*.

(5.) French names, preceded by the article *Le*, *La*, *L'*, are to be recorded under *L*.

Thus: *Le Long (Jacques)*, not *Long (Jacques le)*; *L'Héritier (Marie Jeanne)*, not *Héritier (Marie Jeanne l')*.

(6.) Names with similar prefixes in other languages, are, in all cases, to be recorded under the word following the prefix, with cross-references.

Thus: *Delle Valle*, under *V*; *Della Santa*, under *S*; *Da Cunha* under *C*. So *Buch (Léopold von)*; *Recke (Elisa von der)*; *Dyck (Anton Van)*; *Praet (Joseph Basile Bernard Van)*; *Hooght (Everard van der)*; *Ess (Leander van)*.

XVI. Compound surnames, except Dutch and English, are to be entered under the initial of the first name. In Dutch and in English compound names, the last name is to be preferred.

Thus, in French, such names as *Etienne Geoffroy-Saint-Hilaire*, *Isidore Geoffroy-Saint-Hilaire*, should be written *Geoffroy-Saint-Hilaire (Etienne)*, *Geoffroy-Saint-Hilaire (Isidore)*. So in Spanish, *Calderon de la Barca*, and *Calderon y Belgrano*, should both be entered under *C*. But *François de Salignac de Lamotte Fénélon*, is universally placed under *Fénélon*, even by those who generally adhere to the above rule. There are other names, which must be considered exceptions, respecting which it seems impossible to give any invariable rule, but all difficulty must be removed by cross-references.

XVII. Works of an author who may have changed his name, or added others to it, are to be recorded under the last name, (if used in any of his publications,) with cross-references from the other names. Names that may have been altered by being used in different languages, are to be entered under their original vernacular form. But if an author has never used the vernacular form of his name in his publications, his works are to be recorded under such other form as he may have employed.

Remark 1. Thus, *Alexander Slidell Mackenzie* should be placed under *Mackenzie*, with a cross-reference from *Slidell*. His family name was *Slidell*, but after becoming known as a writer, he assumed the name *Mackenzie*.

*François Marie Aroüet de Voltaire*, under *Voltaire;* because *Voltaire* is a name assumed as a surname. It is not a title, nor commonly considered part of a compound surname.

*Jean Baptiste Poquelin Molière*, under *Molière.* His father's name was *Poquelin*, but he added, himself, the name *Molière*, as *Aroüet* did that of *Voltaire.*

The family name of an individual is to be considered that which he has, or adopts, for himself and his descendants, rather than that which he received from his ancestors,—*his* family name, not *his father's.* Now if a man's name have been changed, by his own act, the name assumed is supposed to be that by which he wishes to be known to his contemporaries, and which he wishes to transmit to posterity. A married woman generally drops her maiden name, and assumes that of her husband. By this, therefore, she should ever after be known. If she published books under her maiden name, and afterwards under her married name, they should all be recorded under her married name, with a cross-reference from the former. It may be that she published only under her maiden name; in this case, her works should be entered under that name, followed by her married name, included within parentheses.

Remark 2. Such changes as are referred to under this rule may generally be indicated by the mode of printing, thus:

MACKENZIE (Alexander SLIDELL).

VOLTAIRE (François Marie AROÜET de).

DACIER (*Mad.* Anne LEFÈVRE).

XVIII. The following classes of persons are to be entered under their first names, or their Christian names:

(1.) Sovereigns, and Princes of sovereign houses.

(2.) Jewish Rabbis, and Oriental writers in general.

(3.) Persons canonized. The family name, when known, is to be added within brackets.

(4.) Friars, who, by the constitution of their order, drop their surnames. But the family name, when known, should be added within brackets.

(5.) All other persons known *only* by their first names, to which, for the sake of distinction, they add those of their native places, profession, rank, &c., as, *Adamus Bremensis*, or *Adam of Bremen.*

A cross-reference should be made from any other name by which the author may be known, to that used as the heading.

XIX. Surnames of Noblemen and Dignitaries, with the exception of cases coming under the preceding rule, are to be ascertained, when not expressed, and to be used for the heading, although the person may be better known by his title, than by his name. But, in all cases where doubt would be likely to arise, cross-references should be used.

REMARK. Thus, *Home (Henry), Lord Kames.* There should be a cross-reference; thus, *Kames (Lord). See Home (Henry). Stanhope (Philip Dormer), Earl of Chesterfield.*

This last is one of the cases which might lead us to doubt the propriety of the rule. This author is universally known as *Chesterfield*, not as *Stanhope*. But there are other authors, who are as well known by their family names as by their titles; while the greater portion are known by their family names, much better than by their titles. A general rule is absolutely necessary, and this is thought to be the best.

XX. If it appear upon the title-page, that the work is the joint production of several writers, it is to be entered under the first named, with cross-references from the names of the others.

XXI. The complete works, or entire treatises of several authors, published together in one series, with a collective title, are to be recorded in the words of the general title of the series, and to be placed under the name of the Editor, if known; if that be not known, under the title of the collection, like anonymous works. If any work in the collection be printed with a separate title-page, and an independent paging, it is also to be recorded under its author's name, as a distinct work, with a reference to the volume of the collection in which it is to be found.

Cross-references may be made from names of authors, when they appear upon the title-page, or when their works were first published in the collection.

Explanation 1. The principle established by this rule, decides the case, common among German books, of *works with double titles*, one general and the other special. Such a work must be entered twice, once under the general title, which should omit, as much as possible, what is contained in the special; and once under the special title, which should refer to the general, stating what volume of the general collection this particular volume forms.

Explanation 2. This rule applies to *periodical publications*, which should be entered under the name of the Editor, if this appears upon the title-page, with a cross-reference from the name of the publication. But if the publication be issued under the direction of an association, it comes under the next rule, and is to be recorded under the name of the association, with a cross-reference from the editor's name.

Remark. The catalogue, thus formed, will be composed of works, having each a distinct title-page and an independent pagination. Doubtless, greater convenience and usefulness might be attained by adopting a more comprehensive plan; — one, by which every distinct article in Transactions of Learned Societies, in Magazines, Reviews, and similar works, where, by the rule of the publication, the authors of the treatises are named,—should be separately entered, as if it were a book. Such an attempt is, however, at present, unadvisable. Should it, hereafter, be thought practicable to extend the rule, none of the titles which have been prepared, under this rule, will be superfluous, and none will have to be altered. It is hoped, that, within a few years, such progress may be made in the General Catalogue, as to justify the attempt at greater minuteness of registration.

XXII. Academies, institutes, associations, universities, colleges; literary, scientific, economical, eleemosynary and religious societies; national and municipal governments; assemblies, conventions, boards, corporations, and other bodies of men, under whatever name, and of whatever character, issuing publications, whether as separate works, or in a continuous series, under a general title, are to be considered and treated as the authors of all works issued by them, and in their name alone. The heading is to be the name of the body, the principal word to be the first word, not an article. A cross-reference is to be made from any important substantive or adjective, to the principal word.

EXPLANATION 1. If the name of the author appears upon the title-page of a work having a distinct title-page and paging, published by such a body, the work then comes under Rule XXI. It must be recorded twice; once under the general title, according to the above rule, and again under the name of the author, referring, if it be published in a series, to the volume of the series in which it is contained.

EXPLANATION 2. Catalogues of public libraries are to be entered under the name of the establishment; and if the name of the compiler appears upon the title-page, a cross-reference should be made from it to the principal entry.

EXPLANATION 3. When committees, or branches of a body, issue publications, the heading is to be the name of the chief, and not of the subordinate body. Thus, under *United States,* would be placed all public documents issued at the expense of the United States, whether as regular Public Documents, or by particular Departments, Bureaus, or Committees. Such titles, when they become numerous, may be classed, and conveniently arranged in the catalogue.

On the same principle, the publications of literary and other societies connected with colleges and universities are to be catalogued under the names of the colleges, &c., with cross-references from the names of the societies.

EXPLANATION 4. Under this rule, Liturgies, Prayer-Books, Breviaries, Missals, &c., are to be placed under the English name of the communion, religious order or denomination, under whose authority they are prepared and published. Similar works by individuals, are to be placed under their names.

XXIII. Translations are to be entered under the heading of the original work, with a cross-reference from the name of the translator. If the name of the translator be known, and that of the author unknown, the book is to be entered, like other anonymous works, under the first word of the original title, not an article or preposition, whether the original be or be not in the library to be catalogued.

When the title of the original cannot be ascertained, or cannot be expressed in English letters, the translation is to be entered as an anonymous work, that is, under the first word of its title, not an article or preposition.

XXIV. Commentaries accompanied by the whole Text, are to be entered under the heading of the original work, with a cross-reference from the name of the commentator. If not accompanied by the Text, they are to be entered under the name of the commentator, with a cross-reference from the name of the author.

XXV. The Bible, or any part of it, in any language, is to be entered under the word "Bible."

Cross-references should be made from the names of the writers, as well as from the names of the several parts of the Bible. Both of these classes of names are to be expressed in the form adopted in the authorized English version.

XXVI. Reports of Trials are to be recorded under the name of the Reporter; or if this be not known, under the first word of the Title. There should also be cross-references, from the names of the plaintiff and of the defendant in a civil suit, and from that of the defendant in a criminal suit.

XXVII. The Respondent or defender in a thesis, is to be considered its author, except when it unequivocally appears to be the work of the Præses.

XXVIII. Pseudonymous works are to be entered under the assumed name, followed by *pseud.;* after which may be given the name of the supposed or reputed author, with (in case of doubt) the word *probably* before it, or ? after it.

But if the author have published any edition, continuation, or supplement under his name, the work is not to be considered pseudonymous. In such case, a cross-reference should be made from the feigned name.

EXPLANATION 1. Under pseudonyms are to be included not only fictitious names, such as *Geoffrey Crayon, Gent.*, assumed by Washington Irving, and abbreviated names, as *A. L. Mil.*, for *A. L. Millin;* but also names concealed in an anagram, as *Nides*, for *Denis;* or formed from the initials of the real name, as *Talvi*, for *Theresa Adolfina Louisa Von Jacob*, and all words used fictitiously as proper names of authors.

EXPLANATION 2. Works falsely attributed, in their titles, to particular persons, are also to be treated as pseudonymous, and entered under the names of the pretended authors, with such notes as may be necessary to prevent mistake; unless some edition has been published under the name of the real author.

EXPLANATION 3. Works published with *initials*, are to be entered under the full name of the author, if he be known to have published any edition with his name; otherwise, under the *last* initial, which is to be supposed to stand for the surname, and the other letter or letters for Christian names. But if the last letter be known to stand for a title, it is not to be used for the heading.

XXIX. Anonymous works are to be entered under the first word of the title, not an article or preposition. Cross-references may be made from all words, in the title, under which such a work would be likely to be sought for, in an alphabetical catalogue.

But if the author have published any edition, continuation, or supplement under his name, the work is not to be considered anonymous.

EXCEPTION 1. An anonymous biography or personal narrative is to be entered under the name of the person, whose life or adventures form the subject of the book, if the name appears upon the title-page. But such works should in all cases be designated as anonymous.

EXCEPTION 2. An anonymous continuation, supplement, appendix or index is to be entered under the heading of the original work.

EXPLANATION 1. A book is not to be considered anonymous, when the name of the author is given in any part of it, or expressed by any distinctive description. In such case, the name of the author is to be inserted in the title, within brackets, and is to be used as the heading.

EXPLANATION 2. If it be known that the book has been *attributed* to a certain person, his name may be inserted in the title, within brackets, with such explanation as shall prevent mistake; and a cross-reference may be made from the name of the reputed author.

EXPLANATION 3. Works in which the author is described by some circumlocution, which does not serve to identify him, are to be considered anonymous.

REMARK. This rule will secure uniformity. It will relieve librarians from an almost incalculable amount of labor, perplexity and dissatisfaction. It will relieve readers from every inconvenience, except that of sometimes being obliged to look in two places for the book. On these accounts, a simple, arbitrary rule is the only one that can safely be adopted. Any rule for selecting the most prominent word of a title, or for entering a book under the name of its subject, would be found fatal to uniformity; it would greatly increase the trouble of making a catalogue; it would not render the catalogue more convenient for readers, but, in the main, much less so. The only objections to the proposed rule are, that it brings many titles under words of little significance, as a "*Brief* Survey", a "*Succinct* Narrative", &c., and that it brings many titles together, under such words as "Essay", "History", "Narrative", &c. These objections have been fully considered, and the rule is given with the settled conviction that the inconveniences alluded to are much less than those which would result from any other rule or set of rules, which have been proposed, or can be devised.

## CROSS-REFERENCES.

XXX. Cross-references,—consisting of only the word from which reference is made, the word *See*, and the name or heading referred to,—are to be made in the following instances:

(1.) From other forms of a name, than the one adopted in the heading.

(2.) From any name used by an author, or by which he may be generally known, other than the one used for the heading.

(3.) From important words in the name of any collective body, used as a heading, under Rule XXII.

(4.) From names of subordinate bodies, when a work is entered under the name of the principal body, under Rule XXII.

(5.) From the name of a supposed author of a pseudonymous work.

(6.) From titles, or designations of office, or dignity, when used upon title-pages, instead of surnames.

(7.) From the family names of persons, whose works are entered under the Christian, or first names; except sovereigns, or princes belonging to sovereign houses.

(8.) From the names of the several parts of the Bible, and of the writers of them.

(9.) From former titles of periodicals, when the publication is catalogued under an altered title, or a new editor, according to Rule VII.

XXXI. The following classes of cross-references, employed to prevent the necessity of entering titles in full, more than once, are to contain so much of the title referred to, as may be necessary to show distinctly the object of the reference. When it would be difficult to abbreviate the title, for this purpose, other words, not those of the title, may be used.

(1.) From the names of Translators, Editors, Commentators, Continuators, or other persons, named on the title-page, (or added to the title, on the principle of Rule XII.), as participating in the authorship of the work.

(2.) From the name of any person, the subject of a biography or narrative.

(3.) From the name of an author, any whole work of whom, or some considerable part of it, may be the subject of any commentary or notes, without the text.

(4.) From the name of an author, whose complete works are contained in any collection, or any considerable part of whose works have been first published in such collection, if the name be given upon the title-page.

(5.) From any word, in the title of an anonymous work, under which one would be likely to seek for the work in an alphabetical catalogue.

(6.) From the name of a supposed author of an anonymous work.

(7.) From the names of the plaintiff and of the defendant, in the report of a civil suit; and from the name of the defendant, in that of a criminal suit.

(8.) From the name of a former editor of a periodical, when the publication is catalogued under the name of a new editor, according to Rule VII.

---

## ARRANGEMENT.

XXXII. The order of the Headings will be determined by the plan of the catalogue, whether alphabetical, classed, or chronological.

XXXIII. The Titles are immediately to follow the headings; and within the divisions and sub-divisions given below, the arrangement is to be chronological. Editions without date, and those of which the date cannot be ascertained, even by approximation, are to precede all those bearing date, or of which the date can be supplied, either positively or by approximation. The latter are to follow, according to their date, whether apparent in any part of the book, or supplied. Editions by the same editor, or such as are expressly stated to follow a specific text or edition, and editions with the same notes or commentary, to succeed each other, in their chronological order, immediately after the entry of that which is, or is considered to be, the earliest.

XXXIV. Titles, which occur under the name of an author, are to be arranged in the following order:

(1.) Collections of all the works.

*a.* Those without translations, whether with or without notes, commentaries, lives, or other critical apparatus.

*b.* Those with translations.

Editions with only one translation. Those with a Latin translation are to be placed first; next those with an English; and then those with a translation into any other language, in the alphabetical order of the English name of such language.

Editions with several translations into different languages. Those are to be entered first, which have the fewest number of translations. Among those having the same number of translations, the alphabetical order of the first of the languages employed is to be followed.

*c.* Translations without the text. These are to be arranged among themselves according to the principles laid down for translations with the text.

(2.) Partial collections, containing two or more works. Those which contain the greatest number of works are to precede. The arrangement of the whole is to be, in other respects, according to the principles laid down for collections of all the works.

(3.) Selections or collected fragments. Those from all the works are to precede those from several works, and the whole to be arranged according to the foregoing principles.

(4.) Separate works. These are to succeed each other alphabetically. Entire portions of a separate work are to follow immediately after the work itself. The different editions and translations are to be arranged according to the foregoing principles.

(5.) Entire portions of a separate work, when the work itself does not occur.

XXXV. Works placed under the names of collective bodies, (according to Rule XXII,) are, in general, to be arranged in alphabetical order; but works forming part of a series are not to be separated, although that series be interrupted, or the title changed; and works published by branches or subordinate bodies, are to be separately arranged and placed under subheadings, which should be printed in a distinctive type.

XXXVI. Cross-References are to be placed after all other entries under the heading, and in alphabetical order of the names referred to.

XXXVII. The entries under the word BIBLE, are to be arranged in the following order; subject in other respects to the principles laid down in Rule XXXIV, except that, in each of the following classes, editions with the text alone are to precede those with commentaries.

(1.) The Old and New Testaments with or without the Apocrypha.

(2.) The Old Testament.

(3.) Detached parts of the Old Testament, in the same order in which they are arranged in the English authorized version of the Scriptures.

(4.) The New Testament.

(5.) Detached parts of the New Testament.

(6.) Apocryphal books.

---

## MAPS, ENGRAVINGS, MUSIC.

XXXVIII. Maps, Charts, Engravings and Music, (except when published in volumes,) are not to be included in catalogues of Books. Separate catalogues of these should be constructed upon the general principles of the preceding rules.

(1.) In cataloguing MAPS AND CHARTS, the full title is to be given, including the names of surveyors, compilers, engravers, publishers, &c.; date and place of publication; and number of sheets composing the map. Each edition is to be separately recorded, and the separate title of each sheet, when it varies from the general title. The titles of sub-sketches are to be introduced at the close of the main title, within brackets, and to be given in full, including authorship, scale and size.

(2.) The scale is to be given in all cases. When not stated on the map, it is, if possible, to be derived from it.

(3.) The size of the map, within the *neat-line* of the border, is to be given in inches and tenths. When a map has no printed border, the measure of the limits of printed surface is to be given.

(4.) The price, if stated on the map, should be copied.

(5.) All important peculiarities of copy, such as the kind of paper, and whether backed, folded, bound, on rollers, &c., should be mentioned in a note.

The titles thus prepared are to be arranged under the names of the countries, or divisions of the earth's surface delineated in the maps; and these names are to be disposed in alphabetical order, with the cross-references necessary to facilitate research.

(6.) ENGRAVINGS are to be recorded under the names of the engravers, with cross-references from those of the painters or designers. The date, and the name of the publisher, if found upon the print, should also be given. The size of the print, in inches and tenths, should also be stated. If the copy be an artists' proof, or a remarkably good impression of a valuable engraving, the fact should be stated in a note.

(7.) MUSIC is to be entered under the name of the composer. If the work have a distinctive title, there should be a cross-reference from that.

## EXCEPTIONAL CASES.

XXXIX. Cases not herein provided for, and exceptional cases, requiring a departure from any of the preceding rules, are to be decided upon by the superintendent.

# EXAMPLES.

(A)

# REMARKS ON THE EXAMPLES.

---

The following examples are introduced, for the purpose of illustrating the rules, and of furnishing specimens of different kinds of titles, as well as of showing the general appearance of the proposed catalogues. In some respects, these are not average specimens; but have been selected, partly on account of their containing difficulties. Some titles would require a large number of cross-references. Only so many are here inserted as are necessary for the purpose of illustration.

It has not been convenient to give examples of titles in languages which use other than Roman letters. Our printing-office is not yet supplied with the requisite variety of type. For the same reason, in some of the titles, words are spelled in full, which, in the books, are printed with signs of abbreviation. There is a branch of this invention which promises to furnish us with the means of engraving, with facility, any desired characters, and of stereotyping them from the engraved plates.

The application of the rules to the examples will, in most cases, be sufficiently obvious, but, it may not be amiss to make some explanations respecting a few of them.

Rule 1 to 3. The examples illustrating these rules need not be specially pointed out. Abridgments are frequent; but the rules for omissions could not be illustrated without giving a great number of full titles, with abridgments of the same. When an author has only one Christian name, the full name is supplied, if not given in the title: when more than one, the initials not given are supplied. Errors in titles, even to accidental faults in punctuation, have been scrupulously copied.

Rule 4. See the titles under *Plinius Secundus* and *Orosius*.

Rule 7. See *North American review*, *American quarterly review* and *Bell*. The last journal, being completed, is catalogued according to the principle of Rule 20, under the first editor's name.

Rule 20. See *Cobbett* and *Nyerup*.

Rule 21. See *Gale* and *Historiæ Augustæ scriptores*.

Rule 21, Expl. 1. See *Ancient Irish histories* and *Autobiography*. Many of the special titles to the latter are omitted.

Rule 22. See *Linnean society*, *Great Britain* and *Massachusetts*.

Rule 22, Expls. 2, 3. See *London library*, *University of Oxford* and *Grenville*. The catalogues of private libraries are placed under the names of the proprietors.

Rule 23. See *Méthode*, *Riqueti* and *Oriental historical mss.*

Rule 28. See *Bombet*, *Gualdi*, *Decanver* and *Voltaire*.

Rule 28, Expl. 3. See *C.*, *La Rochefoucauld* and *M* * * *

Rule 29. See *Mémoires*, *Most* and *Harwood*.

Rule 29, Exc. 1. See *Arc* and *Dubois*.
Rule 29, Exc. 2. See *Bossuet* and *Morgues*.
Rule 29, Expl. 1. See *Barbié du Bocage*.

## INDEX OF SUBJECTS.

An index of subjects, applicable to these titles, has been prepared for the purpose of furnishing a specimen of what is proposed for the catalogue. This general index may be printed separately; being of itself, a compact and convenient guide to the contents of the Library. Such an index affords, as will be seen, the opportunity for making a much more minute and useful classification of titles than is practicable in a classed catalogue.

## LOCAL INDEX.

This is intended to furnish an illustration of the method, described on page 23, of designating the various libraries, where any work is to be found, the title of which is in the catalogue. This index will be an indispensable accompaniment to a general catalogue. The references given in the present case are, for the most part, supposititious.

### ABBREVIATIONS.

Acc't *for* account.
Anag. *for* anagram.
App. *for* appendix.
App'd *for* appended.
B. *for* Band and Bände.
Biogr. *for* biography or biographical.
Cols. *for* columns.
Cont'd *for* contained.
Cont'g *for* containing.
Crit. *for* critical.
D. *for* Deel and Deelen.
Ed. *for* edited or edition.
Fo. *for* folio, the fold of the sheet.
Fol. *for* folio, a leaf, singular or plural.
Hist. *for* history or historical.
In par. cols. *for* in parallel columns.
Introd. *for* introduction.
Irr. *for* irregular.
Marg. notes *for* side marginal notes.
Opp. *for* opposite.
P. *for* part, pars, partie, &c., singular or plural.
pp. *for* pages.
Pref. *for* preface.
Pref'd *for* prefixed.
Pseud. *for* pseudonym.
T. *for* tomus, tome, tomo, &c., singular or plural.
Transl. *for* translated or translation.
V. *for* volume, volumen, &c., singular or plural.

# EXAMPLES.

---

ALEXANDER, *the Great.*

*See* CURTIUS RUFUS (QUINTUS). De rebus gestis ALEXANDRI Magni.

AMERICAN quarterly review (The). V. 1–22. . . .
*Philadelphia,* [1827]–'37. 8° (6.7×3.8) [ 2784 ]

ANCIENT Irish histories.—The works of Spencer, Campion, Hanmer, and Marlebvrrovgh. In two volumes. [4 *pagings.*] . . .
[*Dublin, Hibernia press co.,* 1809.] 8° (6.5×4) [ 2424 ]

ANTONINUS LIBERALIS.

*See* GALE (THOMAS). Historiæ poeticæ scriptores. ANTONINUS Liberalis.

APOLLODORUS, *of Athens.*

APOLLODORI Atheniensis bibliothecae libri tres—Ad codd. mss. fidem recensiti a Chr. G. Heyne [*In the original.*]
*Goettingae,* 1782. 8° (4×2.2) [ 1004 ]

*See* GALE (THOMAS). Historiæ poeticæ scriptores. APOLLODORUS Atheniensis.

*See* HEYNE (C. G.). Ad APOLLODORI Ath. bibliothecam notæ, etc.

ARC (JEANNE D').

Memoirs of JEANNE D'ARC, . . . with the history of her times. In two volumes. [4 *pagings.*] . . .
*London,* 1824. 8° (5.3×3.2) [ 1720 ]

AROUËT (FRANÇOIS MARIE). *See* VOLTAIRE.

AUTOBIOGRAPHY. A collection of the most instructive and amusing lives ever published, written by the parties themselves. With brief introductions, and compendious sequels, carrying on the narrative to the death of each writer. V. 1–33. . . . [40 *pagings.*] *London,* 1826–'32. 12° (4.7 *irr.*×2.6 *irr.*) [ 1255 ]

*Note.*—This collection contains the autobiographies of C. Cibber, D. Hume, W. Lilly, F. M. A. de Voltaire, J. F. Marmontel, R. Drury, G. Whitefield, J. Ferguson, M. Robinson, C. Charke, E. Herbert, Prince Eugène of Savoy, A. F. F. von Kotzebue, J. Creichton, W. Gifford, T. Ellwood, L. Holberg, J. H. Vaux, E. Gibbon, B. Cellini, J. Lackington, T. W. Tone, Friedrike Margravine of Baireuth, G. B. Dodington, C. Goldoni, E. F. Vidocq, M. J. Du Barry, and W. Sampson.

AYSCOUGH (SAMUEL).

A general index to the Monthly review, from its commencement, to the end of the seventieth volume. By the Rev. S[AMUEL] AYSCOUGH, . . . In two volumes. . . .
*London*, 1786. 8° (6.5×3.5) [ 2790 ]

A continuation of the general index to the Monthly review; commencing at the seventy-first, and ending with the eighty-first, volume; completing the first series of that work. . . . Compiled by the Rev. S[AMUEL] AYSCOUGH, . . .
*London*, 1796. 8° (6.5×3.6) [ 2791 ]

AYSCU (EDWARD).

A historie contayning the vvarres, treaties, marriages, and other occurrents betweene England and Scotland, from King William the Conqueror, vntill the happy vnion of them both in our gratious King Iames. With a briefe declaration of the first inhabitants of this island: and what seuerall nations haue sithence setled themselues therein one after an other: [*by* EDWARD AYSCU.] * * *
*London*, 1607. 4° (5.5×3.3) [ 2156 ]

BADEN (GUSTAV LUDVIG).

Dansk-norsk historisk Bibliothek, indeholdende Efterretning om de Skrifter, som bidrage til dansk-norsk Historiekundskab. Ved Dr. GUSTAV LUDVIG BADEN.
*Odense*, 1815. 8° (5.4×3.1) [ 391 ]

BAIREUTH (*Margravine of*). *See* FRIEDRIKE SOPHIE WILHELMINE.

BALFOUR (CLARA LUCAS).

Sketches of English literature, from the fourteenth to the present century. By CLARA LUCAS BALFOUR, . . . * * *
*London*, 1852. 8° (5×3) [ 2646 ]

BANKES (HENRY).

The civil and constitutional history of Rome from its foundation to the age of Augustus. By HENRY BANKES esq. In two volumes. * * * . . . *London*, 1818. 8° (6.1×3 4) [ 1384 ]

BARBIÉ DU BOCAGE (JEAN DENIS).

Recueil de cartes géographiques, plans, vues et médailles de l'ancienne Grèce, relatifs au voyage du jeune Anacharsis, précédé d'une analyse critique des cartes. [*By* J. D. BARBIÉ DU BOCAGE.] Seconde édition.
*Paris*, 1789. 8° (7.3×4.6) *pp. xlij. maps, &c.*, 31. [ 1216 ]

BAREITH (*Margravine of*). *See* BAIREUTH.

BARTHÉLEMY (JEAN JACQUES).

Voyage du jeune Anacharsis en Grèce, dans le milieu du quatrième siècle avant l'ère vulgaire. Seconde édition. T. 1-7. [*By* J. J. BARTHÉLEMY. *With tables in V. 7, pp. cccxxij.*]
*Paris*, 1789. 8° (5.3×3.1) *marg. notes.* [ 1215 ]

*Note.*—For maps, *see* Barbié du Bocage, Jean Denis.

BASNAGE DE BEAUVAL (JACQUES).

The history of the Jews, from Jesus Christ to the present time: . . . Being a supplement and continuation of the history of Josephus. Written in French by Mr. [JACQUES] BASNAGE [DE BEAUVAL]. Translated into English by Tho. Taylor, A. M.
*London*, 1708. *fo.* (12.3×6.9 *irr.*) 2 *cols.* [ 1429 ]

BAYARD (*Chevalier*). *See* DU TERRAIL (PIERRE).

BAZIN (*L'abbé*), *pseud.* *See* VOLTAIRE (F. M. A. DE).

BECKER (WILHELM ADOLF).

Gallus: or, Roman scenes of the time of Augustus; with notes and excursuses illustrative of the manners and customs of the Romans. By Professor W. A. BECKER. Translated by the Rev. Frederick Metcalfe, . . . [*With plates.*]
*London*, 1849. 12° (6.2×3.5) [ 1775 ]

BELISARIUS.

*See* STANHOPE (PHILIP HENRY). Life of BELISARIUS.

BELL (THOMAS), *Sec. R. S.*

The zoological journal. V. 1, 2. From March, 1824, . . . to April, 1826. Conducted by THOMAS BELL, esq. F.L.S. . . . V. 3, 4. From January, 1827, . . . to May, 1829. Edited by N. A. Vigors, . . . [*With plates.*]
*London*, 1825-'29. 8° (6.2×3.6) [ 2940 ]

*Note.*—Mr. Bell was assisted in the publication of V. 1, 2, by J. G. Children, J. De C. Sowerby, and G. B. Sowerby; Mr. Vigors, in the publication of V. 3, 4, by T. Bell, E. T. Bennett, J. E. Bicheno, W. J. Broderip, J. G. Children, Thos. Hardwicke, T. Horsfield, W. Kirby, J. De C. Sowerby, G. B. Sowerby, and W. Yarrell.

BENTINCK (*Lord* GEORGE).

*See* DISRAELI (BENJ.). Biography of Lord GEO. BENTINCK.

BEYLE (HENRI).

*See* BOMBET (L. A. C.), *pseud. for* HENRI BEYLE.

BODLEIAN LIBRARY. *See* UNIVERSITY OF OXFORD.

BOMBET (Louis Alexandre César), *pseud. for Henri Beyle.*

The lives of Haydn [*by G. Carpani,*] and Mozart [*by Schlichtegroll*], with observations on Metastasio, and on the present state of music in France and Italy. Translated from the French of L. A. C. Bombet [*H. Beyle, by R. Brewin*]. With notes, by [*W. Gardiner,*] . . . Second edition.
*London,* 1818. 8° (5.9×3.3) [ 1864 ]

BONAPARTE (Napoléon). *See* NAPOLÉON I. Bonaparte.

BOSSUET (Jacques Bénigne), *Bishop of Meaux.*

Discours sur l'histoire universelle. Pour expliquer la suite de la religion & les changemens des empires. Première partie. Depuis le commencement du monde jusqu'à l'empire de Charlemagne. Par Messire Jacques Bénigne Bossuet, . . . Dixième édition. . . . [*With 3 maps.*]
*Amsterdam,* 1710. 12° (4.9×2) *marg. notes.* [ 1377 ]

Continuation de l'histoire universelle de Messire Jacques Bénigne Bossuet, . . . [*By Jean de La Barre.*] Tome second. Depuis l'an 800. de nôtre Seigneur jusqu'à l'an 1687. inclusivement. [*With 3 maps.*]
*Amsterdam,* 1714. 12° (4.9×2.5) [ 1378 ]

Discours sur l'histoire universelle, à Monseigneur le dauphin: pour expliquer la suite de la religion, et les changemens des empires. Première partie. Depuis le commencement du monde jusqu'à l'empire de Charlemagne. Par Messire Jacques Bénigne Bossuet, . . . Nouvelle édition.
*Paris,* 1752. 12° (4.5 *irr.*×2.1) *marg. notes.* [ 1435 ]

Suite de l'histoire universelle, de Monsieur l'évêque de Meaux [J. B. Bossuet]. Depuis l'an 800. de notre Seigneur jusqu'à l'an 1700. inclusivement. Seconde partie. Nouvelle édition. [*By J. de La Barre.*] *Paris,* 1752. 12° (4.8×2.4) [ 1436 ]

BOWDICH (*Mrs.* T. Ed.). *See* LEE (*Mrs.* R.).

BROTHERS in unity. *See* YALE college.

BULWER (*Sir* Edward Lytton). *See* LYTTON (*Sir* Ed. G. E. L. BULWER).

C. (M. G. D.), *Gatien de Courtilz de Sandras.*

Mémoires de Monsieur de Bordeaux, intendant des finances. Par M. G. D. C. [*Gatien de Courtilz de Sandras.*] T. 1–4.
*Amsterdam,* 1758. 12° (4.7×2.3) [ 2731 ]

CÆSAR (CAIUS JULIUS).

*See* NAPOLÉON I. Précis des guerres de CÉSAR.

CAMPION (EDMUND).

Ancient Irish histories.—A historie of Ireland, written in the yeare 1571. By EDMUND CAMPION, . . . [*Ed. by James Ware.*] *Dublin*, 1809. 8° (6.7×4) [ 2426 ]

*Note.*—Cont'd in V. 1 of "Ancient Irish histories." A reprint of the Dublin edition of 1633.

CAPITOLINUS (JULIUS).

*See* HISTORIÆ Augustæ scriptores. JULIUS CAPITOLINUS.

CASTRO (JOÃO DE).

*See* FREIRE DE ANDRADA (JACINTO). Vida de JOÃO DE CASTRO.

CATTEAU-CALLEVILLE (JEAN PIERRE GUILLAUME).

Histoire de Christine, reine de Suède, avec un précis historique de la Suède depuis les anciens tems jusqu'à la mort de Gustave-Adolphe-le-Grand, . . . par [J. P. G.] CATTEAU-CALLEVILLE, . . . T. 1, 2. *** *Paris*, 1815. 8° (5.7×3.1) [ 1876 ]

CAVENDER (C. H.).

*See* DECANVER (H. C.), *anag. for* C. H. CAVENDER.

CIBBER (COLLEY).

An apology for the life of Mr. COLLEY CIBBER, comedian. Written by himself. *** *London*, 1829. 12° (4.7×2.6) [ 1256 ]

*Note.*—V. 1 of "Autobiography."

CLÉMENT (DAVID).

Bibliothèque curieuse historique et critique, ou catalogue raisonné de livres dificiles à trouver, par DAVID CLÉMENT. T. 1–9. *** *T.* 1–3, *Göttingen*, *T.* 4, 5, *Hannover*, *T.* 6–9, *Leipsic*, 1750–'60 4° (6.5×5) [ 2638 ]

*Note.*—This catalogue is alphabetical, but unfinished, extending only to *Hessus.*

COBBETT (WILLIAM).

Elements of the Roman history, in English and French, from the foundation of Rome to the battle of Actium; selected from the best authors, ancient and modern, with a series of questions . . . The English by WILLIAM COBBETT; the French by J. H. Sievrac. *London*, 1828. 12° (5.5×3.1) [ 1029 ]

*Note.*—With a title-page in French.

COCHRANE (JOHN GEORGE).

*See* LONDON LIBRARY. Catalogue; compiled by J. G. COCHRANE.

CONON Grammaticus.

*See* GALE (Thomas). Historiæ poeticæ scriptores. Conon Grammaticus.

COURTILZ de Sandras (Gatien de).

*See* C. (M. G. D.), Gatien de Courtilz de Sandras.

*See* DU BUISSON (——), *pseud. for* Gatien de Courtilz de Sandras.

CUETO (Leopoldo Augusto de).

*See* QUEYPO de Llano (J. M.). Historia de España: con su vida por L. A. de Cueto.

CURTIUS Rufus (Quintus).

[Q. Curtii Rufi, de rebus gestis Alexandri regis Macedonum libri viii. Pref'd are two books of supplement. App'd are the supplements of J. Freinsheim, pp. 93. Edited by D. Elzevir.]
8° (6.9×3.4) [ 1379 ]

CUVIER (Georges Léopold Chrétien Frédéric Dagobert), *Baron.*

*See* LEE (*Mrs.* R.). Memoirs of G. L. C. F. D. Cuvier.

DECANVER (H. C.), *anagram for C. H. Cavender.*

Catalogue of works in refutation of Methodism, from its origin in 1729, to the present time. Of those by Methodist authors on lay-representation, Methodist episcopacy, etc., etc., and of the political pamphlets relating to Wesley's "Calm address to our American colonies." Compiled by H. C. Decanver [*C. H. Cavender*].
*Philadelphia*, 1846. 8° (6.3×3.8) *pp.* 54. [ 310 ]

DIBDIN (Thomas Frognall).

The bibliomania; or, book-madness; containing some account of the history, symptoms, and cure of this fatal disease. In an epistle addressed to Richard Heber, esq. By the Rev. Thomas Frognall Dibdin, F. S. A. * * *
*London*, 1809. 8° (6.4 *irr.*×3.5) *pp.* 87. [ 2736 ]

The bibliomania; or book-madness; containing some account of the history, symptoms, and cure of this fatal disease. In an epistle addressed to Richard Heber, esq. By the Rev. Thomas Frognall Dibdin, F. S. A. * * *
*London*, [1842.] 8° (6.4×3.6) *pp.* 64. [ 2631 ]

*Note.*—A reprint of "The first edition," 1809.

Bibliomania; or book madness: a bibliographical romance, in six parts. [1 *paging. 2d edition.*] Illustrated with cuts. By the Rev. Thomas Frognall Dibdin. * * *
*London*, 1811. 8° (6.3 *irr.*×3.5) [ 2629 ]

Bibliomania; or book-madness; a bibliographical romance. Illustrated with cuts. By THOMAS FROGNALL DIBDIN, D. D. New and improved edition, to which are now added preliminary observations, and a supplement including a key to the assumed characters in the drama. [*With indexes, pp. xxxiv.*]
*London*, 1842. 8° (6.4×3.7) [ 2630 ]

DIOGENES LAËRTIUS.

DIOGENIS LAERTII de vitis, dogmatibus et apophthegmatibus clarorum philosophorum libri X. Græce et Latine [*in par. cols.*]. Cum subjunctis integris annotationibus Is. Casauboni, Th. Aldobrandini & Mer. Casauboni. Latinam Ambrosii versionem complevit & emendavit Marcus Meibomius. Seorsum excusas Æg. Menagii in Diogenem observationes auctiores habet volumen II. . . . Additæ denique sunt priorum editionum præfationes, & indices locupletissimi. *** [*V.* 1, 2. *With portraits.*]
*Amstelædami*, CIƆ IƆ C VIIIC. 4° (8.1×5.4) [ 1414 ]

DISRAELI (BENJAMIN).

Lord George Bentinck: a political biography. By B[ENJAMIN] DISRAELI, . . . *** Second edition.
*London*, 1852. 8° (5.8×3.3) [ 2757 ]

DISRAELI (ISAAC), *or D'Israeli.*

Amenities of literature; consisting of sketches and characters of English literature, illustrating the literary, political, and religious vicissitudes of the English people. By I[SAAC] D'ISRAELI, . . . In three volumes. . . . Second edition.
*London*, 1842. 8° (6.3×3.6) [ 2622 ]

Curiosities of literature. By ISAAC DISRAELI. With a view of the life and writings of the author. By his son. In three volumes. . . . Fourteenth edition. [*With 2 portraits, a fac-simile, & a view.*] *London*, 1849. 8° (6.7×3.8) [ 2734 ]

DUBOIS (GUILLAUME), *Archbishop of Cambray.*

Vie privée du cardinal [GUILLAUME] DUBOIS, . . . [*By Antoine Mongez.*] *Londres*, 1789. 8° (5.7×3.1) [ 1721 ]

DU BUISSON (——), *pseud. for Gatien de Courtilz de Sandras.*

The history of the life and actions of . . . the Viscount de Turenne. Written in French by Monsieur DU BUISSON [*G. de Courtilz de Sandras*], . . . And translated into English by Ferrand Spence. . . . *London*, 1686. 8° (5.7×3.3) [ 1719 ]

DUMOURIEZ (CHARLES FRANÇOIS DUPERIER).

The life of General [C. F.] DUMOURIEZ. In three volumes. . . . *** *London*, 1796. 8° (6×3.5) [ 1702 ]

DU TERRAIL (PIERRE), *Chevalier Bayard.*

*See* SIMMS (W. G.). Life of PIERRE DU TERRAIL, Chevalier Bayard.

EDINBURGH review (The), or critical journal: . . . quarterly. *** . . . *London.* 8° (6.7×3.8) [ 2781 ]

*Note.*—This publication was commenced in October, 1802. To October, 1853, inclusive, there were published 98 volumes.

General index to the EDINBURGH review, from its commencement in October 1802, to the end of the twentieth volume, published in November 1812. *Edinburgh,* 1813. 8° (6.6×3.8) [ 2782 ]

General index to the EDINBURGH review, from the twenty-first to the fiftieth volumes inclusive. (April 1813 – January 1830.) *Edinburgh,* 1832. 8° (6.8×4) 2 *cols.* [ 2783 ]

EMERSON (GEORGE BARRELL).

*See* MASSACHUSETTS. Report on the trees and shrubs of M.; by G. B. EMERSON.

ESS (WILLEM LODEWYK VAN).

The life of Napoleon Buonaparte; containing . . . a philosophical review of his manners and policy as a soldier, a statesman, and a sovereign: including memoirs and original anecdotes of the imperial family, and the most celebrated characters that have appeared in France during the revolution. By WILLEM LODEWYK VAN ESS. Illustrated with portraits. V. 1–4. *Philadelphia,* 1809, '10. 8° (6.6×3.7) [ 1854 ]

EYTON (THOMAS C.).

A history of the rarer British birds. By T. C. EYTON, esq. Illustrated with woodcuts. *London,* 1836. 8° (6.3×3.6) [ 2893 ]

A catalogue of British birds. By T. C. EYTON, esq. *London,* 1836. 8° (6.3×3.5) *pp.* 67. [ 2894 ]

FRIEDRIKE SOPHIE WILHELMINE, *Margravine of Baireuth.*

Memoirs of FREDERICA SOPHIA WILHELMINA, . . . Margravine of Bareith, sister of Frederic the Great. Written by herself. Translated from the original French. In two volumes. . . . *London,* 1828. 12° (4.6×2.7) [ 1278 ]

*Note.*—V. 20, 21 of "Autobiography."

FREIRE DE ANDRADA (JACINTO).

Vida de D. João de Castro, . . . escrita por JACINTO FREIRE DE ANDRADA. Nova edição emendada, e acrescentada com a vida do autor. *Paris,* 1818. 12° (5×2.6) *marg. notes.* [ 1815 ]

FRONTINUS (Sextus Julius).

Sexti Julii Frontini viri consularis strategematicôn sive de solertibus ducum factis & dictis libri quatuor. Samuel Tennulius variis mss. contulit, emendavit, notis illustravit, & copiosissimo indice rerum ac verborum ornavit. * * *
*Lugduni-Batav. & Amstelædami,* 1675. 12° (4.2×2.1) [ 1053 ]

* * * Astvtie militari di Sesto Iulio Frontino huomo consolare, di tvtti li famosi et eccellenti capitani romani, greci, barbari, et hesterni. [*Ending "Stampato in Vinegia . . . mdxxxvi."*]
1537. 8° (4.9×2.9) * * * [ 1054 ]

GALE (Thomas).

Historiæ poeticæ scriptores antiqui. Apollodorus Atheniensis. Conon Grammaticus. Ptolemæus Hephæst. f. Parthenius Nicaensis. Antoninus Liberalis. Græcè & Latinè. Accessêre breves notæ & indices necessarij. [*Ed. by* Thomas Gale.]
*Parisiis,* 1675. 8° (5.5×3.3) 3 *pagings.* [ 1002 ]

GALLICANUS (Vulcatius).

*See* HISTORIÆ Augustæ scriptores. Vulcatius Gallicanus.

GANDELL (Henry Wood).

*See* VOLTAIRE (F. M. A. de). Philos. of hist.; transl. by H. W. Gandell.

GODDARD (Austin Parke).

*See* GUICCIARDINI (Fr.). History of Italy; transl. by A. P. Goddard.

GODWIN (*Mrs.* Mary W.). *See* WOLLSTONECRAFT (Mary).

GRAHAM (Catharine SAWBRIDGE Macaulay).

The history of England from the accession of James i. . . . to the revolution. V. 1–5 . . . By Catharine Macaulay. V. 6–8. By Catharine Macaulay Graham. [*With an app. to V. 2, pp. xxiv, & to V. 5, pp. lv.*]
*London,* 1763–'83. 4° (7.4×4.7) *marg. notes.* [ 2118 ]

The history of England, from the revolution to the present time, in a series of letters to the Reverend Doctor Wilson, . . . By Catharine Macaulay [Graham]. V. 1.
*Bath,* 1778. 4° (7×4.5) [ 2119 ]

GREAT BRITAIN.

State papers published under the authority of his majesty's commission. V. 1–11. King Henry the Eighth. . . . [*With 3 genealog. tables & 3 maps.*]
[*London,*] 1831–'52. 4° (8.1×5.5) *marg. notes.* [ 2296 ]

GRENVILLE (THOMAS).

Bibliotheca Grenvilliana; or bibliographical notices of rare and curious books, forming part of the library of the Right Hon. THOMAS GRENVILLE: by John Thomas Payne and Henry Foss. V. 1, 2. [1 *paging. Alphabetical; with an index, pp. xxxiii, & addenda.*] *London*, 1842. 8° (6.9×3.9) 2 *cols.* [ 2737 ]

Bibliotheca Grenvilliana; part the second, completing the catalogue of the library bequeathed to the British museum by the late Right Hon. THOMAS GRENVILLE. By John Thomas Payne and Henry Foss. [*Alphabetical; with an index, pp. xlii, addenda, & books printed for clubs and societies.*] *London*, 1848. 8° (6.9×3.9) 2 *cols.* [ 2738 ]

GUALDI (*L'abbé*), *pseud. for Gregorio Leti.*

La vie de Madame Olimpe Maldachini qui a gouuerné l'église, durant le pontificat d'Innocent X. c'est à dire, depuis l'an 1644. iusques à l'an 1655. Escrite par l'abbé GVALDI. [*Gregorio Leti.*] *Cosmopoli*, 1666. 12° (4.2×2.3) [ 2700 ]

GUICCIARDINI (FRANCESCO).

The history of Italy, translated from the Italian of FRANCESCO GUICCIARDINI, by Austin Parke Goddard, esq; The third edition. . . . V. 1-10. [*Pref'd to V. 1 is a life of the author, pp. xxxii. App'd to V. 10 is an index, pp. 77.*] *London*, 1763. 8° (5.6×3) *marg. notes.* [ 1600 ]

HANMER (MEREDITH).

Ancient Irish histories.—The chronicle of Ireland. Collected by MEREDITH HANMER, doctor of diuinity, in the yeare 1571. *Dublin*, 1809. 8° (6.7×4) [ 2427 ]

*Note.*—Cont'd in V. 2 of "Ancient Irish histories." A reprint of the Dublin edition of 1633.

HARWOOD (EDWARD).

Biographia classica: the lives and characters of all the classic authors, the Grecian and Roman poets, historians, orators, and biographers. . . . [*By* EDWARD HARWOOD.] The second edition, corrected and improv'd. To which is now added, at the end of every life, a list of the best and most curious editions of each classic author. In two volumes. *London*, 1750. 12° (5.1×2.8) [ 1019 ]

Biographia classica: the lives and characters of the Greek and Roman classics. A new edition, corrected and enlarged, with some additional lives; and a list of the best editions of each author. By EDWARD HARWOOD, D. D. In two volumes. . . . *London*, 1778. 12° (5×2.8) [ 1020 ]

HERCULANO (A.).

Historia de Portugal por A. HERCULANO T. 1–3
*Lisboa*, 1846–'49. 8° (6×3.6) [ 1621 ]

HEYNE (CHRISTIAN GOTTLOB).

Ad Apollodori Atheniensis bibliothecam notae avctore CHR. G. HEYNE cvm commentatione de Apollodoro argvmento et consilio operis et cvm Apollodori fragmentis. P. 1–3. [1 *paging*.]
*Goettingae*, 1783. 8° (4.1×2.4) [ 1006 ]

HISTORIÆ Augustæ scriptores VI. Ælius Spartianus. Julius Capitolinus. Ælius Lampridius. Vulc. Gallicanus. Trebell. Pollio. Flavius Vopiscus. Cum integris notis Isaaci Casauboni, Cl. Salmasii & Jani Gruteri. Cum indicibus locupletissimis rerum ac verborum. T. 1, 2. * * *
*Lugduni Batav*[*orum*], 1671. 8° (5.9×3.4) [ 1201 ]

HUME (DAVID).

The history of England by DAVID HUME, in eight volumes. . . . * * * [*With portraits.*]
*Oxford*, 1826. 8° (6.6×3.5) *marg. notes.* [ 2219 ]

*Note.*—Pref'd to V. 1 are an autobiography of Hume, & a letter from Adam Smith to Wm. Strahan, pp. xxvi.

The life of DAVID HUME. Written by himself.
*London*, 1826. 12° (4.7×2.6) *pp.* 16. [ 1257 ]

*Note.*—V. 2 of "Autobiography."

IRVING (DAVID).

The lives of the Scotish poets, with preliminary dissertations on the literary history of Scotland, and the early Scotish drama. By DAVID IRVINE, L.L.D. [IRVING.] V. 1, 2. [*With* 2 *portraits.*]
*Edinburgh*, 1810. 8° (5.8×3.3) [ 2455 ]

*Note.*—A second copy, in the Library of Congress, purports to be the "Second edition, improved," printed in "London." The only difference is in the title-page.

IRVING (WASHINGTON).

Chronicle of the conquest of Granada. [*By* WASHINGTON IRVING.] From the mss. of Fray Antonio Agapida.
*New-York*, 1850. 12° (5.7×3.5) [ 1816 ]

*Note.*—V. 14 of "The works of Washington Irving."

JERDAN (WILLIAM).

The autobiography of WILLIAM JERDAN, . . . With his literary, political, and social reminiscences and correspondence during the last fifty years. V. 1, 2. [*With* 2 *portraits.*]
*London*, 1852. 8° (5.3×3.1) [ 2479 ]

JERVIS (HENRY JERVIS-WHITE).

History of the island of Corfú, and of the republic of the Ionian islands. By HENRY JERVIS-WHITE JERVIS, . . . *London*, 1852. 12° (5.2×3) [ 1489 ]

JULIANUS (FLAVIUS CLAUDIUS).

*See* LA BLETTERIE (JEAN PH. RENÉ DE). Life of the Emperor JULIAN.

KELLY (MICHAEL).

Reminiscences of MICHAEL KELLY, of the King's theatre, and theatre royal Drury Lane, including a period of nearly half a century; with original anecdotes of many distinguished persons, political, literary, and musical. [*With an app. cont'g an acc't of the King's theatre.*] *New-York*, 1826. 8° (6×3.6) [ 2556 ]

KRAFT (JENS EDVARD).

*See* NYERUP (RAS.). Litteraturlexicon for Danmark, Norge, og Island; ved R. N. og J. E. KRAFT.

LA BARRE (JEAN DE).

*See* BOSSUET (J. B.). Suite de l'hist. univ.; par JEAN DE LA BARRE.

LA BLETTERIE (JEAN PHILIPPE RENÉ DE).

The life of the emperor Julian. Translated from the French [*of* J. P. R. DE LA BLETTERIE.] And improved with coins, notes and a genealogical table. * * * *London*, 1746. 12° (5.1×2.6) [ 1114 ]

LAIRESSE (GERARD DE).

Het groot schilderboek, door GERARD DE LAIRESSE, D. 1, 2. [*With plates.*] *Amsterdam*, 1707. 4° (6.2×4.1) *marg. notes.* [ 644 ]

LAMARTINE (ALPHONSE DE PRAT DE).

The history of the restoration of monarchy in France. By ALPHONSE DE LAMARTINE. . . . V. 1–3. Second edition. *London*, 1851, '52. 8° (5.8×3.3) [ 1748 ]

*Note.*—The edition of V. 2, 3 is not designated.

LAMPRIDIUS (ÆLIUS).

*See* HISTORIÆ Augustæ scriptores. ÆLIUS LAMPRIDIUS.

LA ROCHEFOUCAULD (FRANÇOIS VI. DE), *Duke.*

Mémoires de la minorité de Louis XIV, corrigés & augmentés de plusieurs choses fort considérables, qui manquent dans les autres éditions. Avec une préface nouvelle, qui sert d'indice & de sommaire. Par M. le duc [FRANÇOIS VI.] D[E] L[A] R[OCHEFOUCAULD.] T. 1, 2. *Trévoux*, 1754. 12° (3.9×2.1) [ 2711 ]

LA TOUR D'AUVERGNE (HENRI DE), *Viscount de Turenne.*

*See* DU BUISSON (——). Life of HENRI DE LA TOUR D'AUVERGNE, Viscount de Turenne.

LA TROUSSIÈRE (——).

Mémoires de la vie de François Dusson, . . . Où l'on voit tout ce qui s'est passé de plus considérable, pendant les derniers troubles de France, au sujet de la religion. [*P.* 1, 2. *By* ——LA TROUSSIÈRE.] *Amsterdam*, 1677. 12° (3.9×2.2) [ 2707 ]

LEE (*Mrs.* R.), *formerly Mrs. T. E. Bowdich.*

Memoirs of Baron Cuvier. By Mrs. R. LEE (formerly Mrs. T. Ed. Bowdich). [*With a fac-simile letter.*]
*London*, 1833. 8° (5.8×3.3) [ 1710 ]

LETI (GREGORIO).

*See* GUALDI, (*L'abbé*), *pseud. for* GREGORIO LETI.

LILLY (WILLIAM).

WILLIAM LILLY'S history of his life and times, from the year 1602 to 1681. Written by himself, in the sixty-sixth year of his age, to his worthy friend, Elias Ashmole, esq. Published from the original ms. London, 1715.
*London*, 1829. 12° (4.6×2.6) [ 1258 ]

*Note.*—V. 2 of "Autobiography."

LINNEAN SOCIETY OF LONDON.

The transactions of the LINNEAN SOCIETY OF LONDON. . . . *** [*With plates.*] *London.* 4° (7×5.2 & 7.5×5.5) [ 2825 ]

*Note.*—This publication was commenced in 1791. To 1851, there were published 20 volumes. Pref'd to V. 7 are the charter, bye-laws, &c. of the society, pp. xl. App'd to V. 17 are lists of the members of the society, for 1835 & 1837, pp. 15, each; to V. 18, lists for 1838, 1839, & 1841, pp 15, each. V. 5–20 contain lists of the additions to the library; & V. 10–20, lists of objects presented to the museum.

LINONIAN SOCIETY. *See* YALE COLLEGE.

LONDON LIBRARY.

Catalogue of the LONDON LIBRARY, 12, St. James's square, by. John George Cochrane, . . . The second edition, greatly enlarged. [*Alphabetical; with addenda.*]
*London*, 1847. 8° (6.9×4) [ 2742 ]

LOUIS XIV., *of France.*

*See* LA ROCHEFOUCAULD (FR. VI. DE). Mémoires de la minorité de LOUIS XIV.

LUDEN (HEINRICH).

Geschichte des teutschen Volkes. Von HEINRICH LUDEN. B. 1–12. *** *Gotha*, 1825–'37. 8° (6.1×3.5) [ 1858 ]

LYNES (JOHN).

*See* PARR (SAM.). Catalogue of Parr's library; compiled by JOHN LYNES.

LYTTON (*Sir* EDWARD GEORGE EARLE LYTTON BULWER).

Athens its rise and fall with views of the literature, philosophy, and social life of the Athenian people. By EDWARD [G. E.] LYTTON BULWER [LYTTON], . . . V. 1, 2.
*London,* 1837. 8° (5.8×3.3) [ 1147 ]

M * * * (*Countess de*), *Henriette Julie de Murat.*

Mémoires de Madame la comtesse de M * * *, [*H. J. de Murat,*] avant sa retraite. Servant de réponse aux Mémoires de M. le comte de * * *, rédigés par Monsieur de Saint-Évremond. Nouvelle édition. [*Amsterdam?*] 1753. 12° (4.2×2.2) [ 2733 ]

MACAULAY (CATHARINE). *See* GRAHAM (C. S. M.).

MADDEN (R. R.).

The united Irishmen, their lives and times. By R. R. MADDEN, . . . . *** In two volumes. . . .
*London,* 1842. 12° (5.9×3.2) [ 2440 ]

The united Irishmen, their lives and times. By R. R. MADDEN, M. D. With numerous original portraits. *** Second series. In two volumes. . . . [*With a hist. introd., pp. c, & a map.*]
*London,* 1843. 12° (5.9×3.2) [ 2441 ]

The united Irishmen; their lives and times. By R. R. MADDEN, . . . With numerous original portraits. *** Third series. In three volumes. . . . *Dublin,* 1846. 12° (5.7×3.2) [ 2442 ]

MAHON (*Lord*). *See* STANHOPE (PHILIP HENRY).

MAIDALCHINI (OLIMPIA). *See* PAMFILI (O. M.)

MALDACHINI (OLIMPIA). *See* MAIDALCHINI.

MARCHAND (LOUIS JOSEPH MARIE).

*See* NAPOLÉON I. Précis des guerres de César, écrit avec une préface par L. J. M. MARCHAND.

MARLEBOROUGH (HENRY).

Ancient Irish histories.—The chronicle of Ireland. By HENRY MARLEBVRROVGH; continued from the collection of Doctor Meredith Hanmer, in the yeare 1571.
*Dublin,* 1809. 8° (6.7×4) *pp.* 32. [ 2428 ]

*Note.*—Cont'd in V. 2 of "Ancient Irish histories." A reprint of the Dublin edition of 1633.

MASSACHUSETTS.

A report on the trees and shrubs growing naturally in the forests of MASSACHUSETTS. [*By George B. Emerson.*] Published agreeably to an order of the legislature, by the commissioners on the zoological and botanical survey of the state. [*With 17 plates.*]
*Boston*, 1846. 8° (6.6×3.9) [ 2771 ]

MÉMOIRES sur le consulat. 1799 à 1804. Par un ancien conseiller d'état. *Paris*, 1827. 8° (5.6×3.2) [ 1967 ]

MEN (The) of the time in 1852 or sketches of living notables . . .
*London*, 1852. 16° (4.5×2.8) [ 1828 ]

MEN (The) of the time or sketches of living notables . . .
*New York*, 1852. 12° (5.6×3.3) [ 1948 ]

METCALFE (FREDERICK).

*See* BECKER (W. A.). Gallus; transl. by FRED. METCALFE.

MÉTHODE pour apprendre facilement l'histoire romaine, avec une chronologie du règne des empereurs, & un abrégé des coûtumes des Romains. Nouvelle édition, corrigée & augmentée.
*Londres*, 1754. 24° (4.9×2.7) [ 1069 ]

An easy METHOD of learning the Roman history; with a chronology of the Roman emperors, and an abridged account of the Roman usages and customs. . . . Translated from the French, with additions, by George Watterston, . . .
*Washington*, 1820. 12° (5.4×3.1) [ 1070 ]

MICALI (GIUSÊPPE).

L'Italia avanti il dominio dei Romani [*By* GIUSÊPPE MICALI.] T. 1–4. *Firenze*, 1810. 8° (5.6×3.2) [ 1596 ]

Antichi monumenti per servire all'opera intitolata L'Italia avanti il dominio dei Romani [*By* GIUSÊPPE MICALI.]
*Firenze*, 1810 *fo* (13.2×9.1) *pp. xi. 1 map & 60 plates.* [ 1771 ]

MIRABEAU (*Count de*). *See* RIQUETI (H. G.).

MOLBECH (CHRISTIAN).

Forelæsninger over den nyere danske Poesie, særdeles efter Digterne Evalds, Baggesens og Oehlenschlägers Værker, af CHRISTIAN MOLBECH, . . . Deel 1-2.
*Kiöbenhavn*, 1832. 8° (5.4×3.1) [ 292 ]

Om offentlige Bibliotheker, Bibliothekarer, og det, man har kaldet Bibliotheksvidenskab af CHRISTIAN MOLBECH, . . . (Andet, med et Tillæg og Register forögede Aftryk.)
*Kiöbenhavn*, 1829. 8° (6×3.5) [ 291 ]

Ueber Bibliothekswissenschaft oder Einrichtung und Verwaltung öffentlicher Bibliotheken von CHRISTIAN MOLBECH, . . . Nach der zweiten Ausgabe des dänischen Originals übersetzt von H. Ratjen, . . . Von dem Verfasser mit Zusätzen, mit einem Verzeichnisse der Pergament-drucke der grossen K. Kopenh. Bibliothek und einem Beitrage zur Geschichte dieser Bibliothek vermehrt; von dem Uebersetzer mit Anmerk. versehen. Mit einer Steindrucktafel. *Leipzig*, 1833. 8° (6.2×3.5) [ 317 ]

MONGEZ (ANTOINE).

*See* DUBOIS (GUILL.). Vie privée; par ANT. MONGEZ.

MONTHLY review (The). . . . . *** V. 1–81. V. 1–108. [*New series.*] V. 1–15. New and improved series. V. 1–[33.] New and improved series. *London*, [1809]–'42. 8° (6.6×4) [ 2789 ]

*Note.*—From January, 1831, to December, 1841, inclusive, there was published, annually, a new series of 3 volumes, each. For an index to the first series, *see* Ayscough, Samuel.

A general index to the MONTHLY review, from the commencement of the new series, in January, 1790, to the end of the eighty-first volume, completed in December, 1816. In two volumes. . . . *London*, 1818. 8° (6.8×3.6) [ 2780 ]

MORGUES (MATTHIEU DE), *Sieur de Saint Germain.*

Diverses pièces povr la défence de la royne mère dv roy très-chrestien Lovys XIII. faites et reveves par Messire MATTHIEV DE MORGVES sieur de S. Germain, . . . [*Antwerp?*] 1643. 8° (5.5×2.8) *marg. notes.* [ 2728 ]

Pièces cvrievses povr la deffence de la royne mère dv roy Lovys XIII. par divers avthevrs en suitte de celles du sieur de S. Germain [MATTHIEU DE MORGUES]. . . . T. 2. [*Paris*, 1644?] *Iouxte la copie imprimée à Anuers.* 8° (5.4 *irr.*×2.9) 6 *pagings.* [ 2729 ]

MOST excellent and perfecte homish apothecarye or homely physick booke (A), for all the grefes and diseases of the bodye. Translated out the Almaine speche into English by Jhon Hollybush. *** *Collen*, 1561. *fo.* (8.6×5.2) *marg. notes. fol.* 41. [ 2806 ]

MURAT (HENRIETTE JULIE DE CASTELNAU DE), *Countess.*

*See* M * * * (*Countess de*), H. J. DE MURAT.

NAPOLÉON I. BONAPARTE, *of France.*

Précis des guerres de César, par NAPOLÉON, écrit [*with preface*] par M. Marchand, à l'île Sainte-Hélène, sous la dictée de l'empereur; suivi de plusieurs fragmens inédits. *Paris*, 1836. 8° (5.6×3.3) 1 *chart.* [ 1288 ]

*See* ESS (W. L. VAN). Life of NAPOLEON.
*See* NORVINS (J. M. DE M. DE). Histoire de NAPOLÉON.

NECKER (JACQUES).

De la révolution françoise, par M. [JACQUES] NECKER. T. 1–4.
[*Paris?*] 1796. 8° (5.5×3.1) [ 2070 ]

NORTH AMERICAN review (The). . . . *** [*Quarterly.*]
*Boston.* 12° (6.5×3.5) [ 2778 ]

*Note.*—This publication was commenced in May, 1815. To April, 1853, inclusive, there were published 76 volumes. The titles of V. 1–12 read "The North American review and miscellaneous journal." V. 1–58 are in 8vo. V. 59–76 are in 12mo.

General index to the NORTH AMERICAN review, from its commencement in 1815 to the end of the twenty-fifth volume, published in October, 1827. *Boston,* 1829. 8° (6.1×3.6) [ 2779 ]

NORVINS (JACQUES MARQUET DE MONTBRETON DE).

Histoire de Napoléon, par M. [J. M. DE M.] DE NORVINS. Ornée de portraits, vignettes, cartes et plans. T. 1–4.
*Paris,* 1827, '28. 8° (5.5×3.2) [ 1707 ]

Histoire de Napoléon par M. [J. M. DE M.] DE NORVINS 21e édition illustrée par Raffet *Paris,* 1852. 8° (10×7.2) 2 *cols.* [ 2099 ]

NYERUP (RASMUS).

Almindeligt Litteraturlexicon for Danmark, Norge, og Island; eller Fortegnelse over danske, norske, og islandske, saavel afdöde som nu levende Forfattere, med Anförelse af deres vigtigste Levnets-Omstoendigheder og Liste over deres Skrifter. Ved R. NYERUP og J. E. Kraft.
*Kjöbenhavn,* 1820. (7.5×6) 2 *cols.* [ 216 ]

ORIENTAL historical manuscripts, in the Tamil language: translated; with annotations. By William Taylor, missionary. In two volumes, . . . [*With appendixes A–G., pp.* 52.]
*Madras,* 1835. 4° (7.5×5.6) [ 1410 ]

OROSIUS (PAULUS).

PAULI OROSII historiographi clarissimi opus prestantissimum. *** . . . [*Ending*] Pauli Orosii viri præclarissimi historiarum opus absolutum est: *quod* diligentissime emendatu*m* impressum Parhisiis in Bellouisu pro Ioanne Petit commora*n*te in vico diui Iacobi sub leone argenteo. Anno ab incarnatione Domini. M.CCCCCVI. die. xxi. mensis Ianuarii.
4° (6×3.8) *marg. notes. fol. cxxiii.* [ 1202 ]

PAMFILI (OLIMPIA MAIDALCHINI).

*See* GUALDI (*L'abbé*). La vie d'OLIMPE PAMFILI.

PARR (SAMUEL), *LL.D.*

Bibliotheca Parriana.—A catalogue of the library of . . . SAMUEL PARR, . . . [*Compiled by John Lynes; with a portrait of Parr. Classed, with an alphabetical index, pp. viii.*]
*London*, 1827. 8° (6.4 *irr.*×3.7) [ 2659 ]

PARTHENIUS, *of Nicæa.*

*See* GALE (THOMAS). Historiæ poeticæ scriptores. PARTHENIUS Nicaensis.

PATERCULUS (CAIUS, *or* M. *or* P. VELLEIUS).

C. VELLEIVS PATERCVLVS cvm animadversionibvs Ivsti LipsI, qvas postremvm avxit et emendavit. *** [*With index.*]
*Antverpiæ*, 1667. *fo.* (11.4×6.7) *marg. notes. pp.* 84. [ 1427 ]

PLINIUS SECUNDUS (CAIUS).

[*Beginning, folio* 4, *verso,*] CAII PLYNII SECVNDI natvralis historiae liber .1. [*Ending,*] Caii Plynii Secvndi natvralis historiae libri tricesimiseptimi et vltimi finis impressi Tervisii dvctv et impensis Michaelis Manzoli Parmensis. M.CCCC.LXXIX.
*fo.* (8.3×5.2) 358 *leaves.* [ 2851 ]

POLLIO (TREBELLIUS).

*See* HISTORIÆ Augustæ scriptores. TREBELL. POLLIO.

POTTER (JOHN).

Archæologia Græca: or, the antiquities of Greece. The seventh edition. By JOHN POTTER, . . . V. 1, 2. . . . ***
*London*, 1751. 8° (6.4×3.5 *irr.*) [ 1162 ]

PTOLEMÆUS CHENNUS, *of Alexandria.*

*See* GALE (THOMAS). Historiæ poeticæ scriptores. PTOLEMÆUS.

QUEYPO DE LLANO (JOSÉ MARIA), *Count of Toreno.*

Historia del levantamiento, guerra y revolucion de España, por [J. M. QUEYPO DE LLANO] el conde de Toreno. Nueva edicion aumentada con su vida [*by L. A. de Cueto, pp. l,*] y retrato. T. 1–3.
*Paris*, 1851. 8° (6.8×3.7) [ 2003 ]

RAFFLES (*Sir* THOMAS STAMFORD).

The history of Java. By THOMAS STAMFORD RAFFLES, . . . In two volumes. With a map and plates. . . . [*With app. A–M, pp. cclx.*] *London*, 1817. 4° (7.6×5.3) *marg. notes.* [ 1584 ]

RIQUETI (HONORÉ GABRIEL), *Count de Mirabeau.*

Histoire secrète de la cour de Berlin, ou correspondance d'un voyageur françois, depuis le mois de juillet 1786 jusqu'au 19 janvier 1787. Ouvrage posthume. Avec une lettre remise au roi de Prusse regnant, le jour de son avénement au trône: par le comte de Mirabeau [H. G. RIQUETI]. T. 1, 2.
*Londres,* 1789. 8° (5.5×2.9) [ 2039 ]

The secret history of the court of Berlin; . . . In a series of letters, translated from the French. A posthumous work. To which is added a memorial, presented to the present king of Prussia, on the day of his accession to the throne, by Count Mirabeau [H. G. RIQUETI.] V. 1, 2.
*London,* 1789. 8° (5.7×3.1) [ 2040 ]

SCHELTEMA (JACOBUS).

Staatkundig Nederland; een woordenboek tot de biographische kaart van dien naam, door Mr. JACOBUS SCHELTEMA. D. 1, 2. . . . *Amsterdam,* 1805, '6. 8° (5.6×3) *marg. notes.* [ 645 ]

SIEVRAC (JEAN HENRI).

*See* COBBETT (WM.). Roman hist. in French and English; the Fr. by J. H. SIEVRAC.

SIMMS (WILLIAM GILMORE).

The life of the Chevalier Bayard; "The good knight," "Sans peur et sans reproche." By W. GILMORE SIMMS. ***
*New York,* 1847. 12° (5.7×3.2) [ 1723 ]

SPARTIANUS (ÆLIUS).

*See* HISTORIÆ Augustæ scriptores. ÆLIUS SPARTIANUS.

SPENCE (FERRAND).

*See* DU BUISSON (——). Life of Turenne; transl. by FERRAND SPENCE.

SPENSER (EDMUND).

Ancient Irish histories.—A view of the state of Ireland, written dialogue-wise, betweene Eudoxus and Irenæus. By EDMUND SPENCER, esq. in the yeare 1596. [*Ed. by James Ware.*]
*Dublin,* 1809. 8° (6.5×4) [ 2425 ]

*Note.*—Cont'd in V. 1 of "Ancient Irish histories." A reprint of the Dublin edition of 1633.

STANHOPE (PHILIP HENRY), *Lord Mahon.*

History of the war of the succession in Spain. By [P. H. STANHOPE,] Lord Mahon. Second edition. [*With a map & an app., pp. cxxxv.*] *London,* 1836. 8° (6.3×3.5) [ 1630 ]

The life of Belisarius. By [P. H. STANHOPE,] Lord Mahon. [*With a map.*] *London*, 1829. 8° (6.1×3.5) [ 1304 ]

TACITUS (CAIUS CORNELIUS).

CORNELII TACITI opera. Ad codices antiqvos exacta et emendata commentario critico et exegetico illvstrata edidit Franciscvs Ritter . . . V. 1–4. [*With a biogr. and crit. preface.*] *Cantabrigiae*, 1848. 8° (6.6×3.7) [ 2273 ]

CORNELII TACITI annales. Ad codices antiqvos exacti et emendati commentario critico et exegetico illvstrati opera Francisci Ritteri. V. 1, 2. *Cantabrigiae*, 1848. 8° (6.6×3.7) [ 2274 ]

*Note.*—V. 1, 2 of "Cornelii Taciti opera."

CORNELII TACITI historiae. Ad codices antiqvos exactae et emendatae commentario critico et exegetico illvstratae opera Francisci Ritteri. *Cantabrigiae*, 1848. 8° (6.6×3.7) [ 2275 ]

*Note.*—V. 3 of "Cornelii Taciti opera."

CORNELII TACITI libri minores Germania Agricola Dialogvs. Ad codices antiqvos exacti et emendati commentario critico et exegetico illvstrati opera Francisci Ritteri. Accesservnt indices. *Cantabrigiae*, 1848. 8° (6.6×3.7) [ 2276 ]

*Note.*—V. 4 of "Cornelii Taciti opera."

TAYLOR (WILLIAM).

*See* ORIENTAL hist. mss. in the Tamil language; transl. with annotations by WM. TAYLOR.

THIBAUDEAU (ANTOINE CLAIRE).

Histoire des états généraux et des institutions représentatives en France depuis l'origine de la monarchie jusqu'à 1789 par A. C. THIBAUDEAU [*T*] 1–3. *Bruxelles*, 1844. 8° (6.6×4) [ 2005 ]

THORTSEN (CARL ADOLPH).

Historisk Udsigt over den danske Litteratur indtil Aar 1814. Af Dr. CARL ADOLPH THORTSEN, . . . *Kjöbenhavn*, 1839. 8° (6.2×3.4) [ 290 ]

TORENO (*Count of*). *See* QUEYPO DE LLANO (J. M.).

TOWNSEND (WILLIAM C.).

The lives of twelve eminent judges of the last and of the present century. By WILLIAM C. TOWNSEND, . . . In two volumes. . . . *London*, 1846. 8° (6.6×3.7) [ 2332 ]

TURENNE (*Viscount de*). *See* LA TOUR D'AUVERGNE (HENRI DE).

UNGEWITTER (FRANCIS H.).

Europe, past and present: a comprehensive manual of European geography and history; with separate descriptions and statistics of each state, and a copious index, . . . By FRANCIS H. UNGEWITTER, LL.D. *New York*, 1850. 12° (5.6×3.5) [ 1490

UNIVERSITY OF OXFORD.

Catalogus librorum impressorum bibliothecæ Bodleianæ in ACADEMIA OXONIENSI. V. 1–3.
*Oxonii*, 1843. *fo.* (11.9×7.1) 2 *cols.* [ 140 ]

*Note.*—This catalogue, prepared by Dr. Bulkley Bandinel, contains the titles of books in the library up to 1835, except those of which special catalogues had been published, viz.: Books bequeathed by R. Gough, Books and MSS. bequeathed by F. Douce, "Dissertationes Academicae" [*See* titles of these catalogues below], and those described in the following catalogue, "Bibliotheca celeberrima Hebraca quam collegit Dav. Oppenheimerus, 8° Hamburgi 1820."

Catalogus impressorum librorum quibus aucta est bibliotheca Bodleiana, annis MDCCCXXXV-MDCCCXLVII.
*Oxonii*, 1851. *fo.* (11.8×7.1) 2 *cols.* [ 141 ]

*Note.*—The half-title reads: "Catalogi impressorum librorum bibliothecæ Bodleianæ volumen quartum." It is also designated in the signatures as Vol. 4.

A catalogue of the books, relating to British topography, and Saxon and northern literature, bequeathed to the Bodleian library, in the year MDCCXCIX. by Richard Gough, esq. F. S. A.
*Oxford*, 1814. 4° (7.2×5.3) [ 142 ]

Catalogue of early English poetry and other miscellaneous works illustrating the British drama, collected by Edmond Malone, esq. and now preserved in the Bodleian library. [*Prefixed is a biographical memoir of Edmond Malone.*]
*Oxford*, 1836. *fo.* (11.9×7.1) 2 *cols.* [ 145 ]

Catalogue of the printed books and manuscripts bequeathed by Francis Douce, esq. to the Bodleian library.
*Oxford*, 1840. *fo.* (11.9×7.1) 2 *cols.* [ 144 ]

*Note.*—The Catalogue of manuscripts is separately paged,—90 pages, with 4 lithographic plates.

VAN ESS (WILLEM LODEWYK). *See* ESS.

VOLNEY (CONSTANTIN FRANÇOIS CHASSEBŒUF DE).

Recherches nouvelles sur l'histoire ancienne. P. 1–3, . . . Édition revue et complète. [*By* C. F. C. DE VOLNEY. *With maps & tables.*]
*Paris*, 1814, '15. 8° (5.6×3.4) [ 1154 ]

VOLTAIRE (FRANÇOIS MARIE AROÜET DE).

Memoirs of the life of [F. M. A. DE] VOLTAIRE. Written by himself. With introduction and sequel, condensed from the life by Condorcet. *London*, 1826. 12° (4.6×2.6) [ 1259 ]

*Note.*—V. 2 of "Autobiography."

The philosophy of history, or a philosophical and historical dissertation, on the origin, manners, customs, and religion of the different nations, and people, of antiquity; with a clear and concise exposition, of the usages, and opinions common amongst them; and, in particular, of their religious rites, ceremonies, and superstitions: . . . Translated from the original French manuscripts of Monsr. l'abbé Bazin [*pseud. for* F. M. A. DE VOLTAIRE]. By Henry Wood Gandell, . . . ***
*London*, 1829. 8° (6.2×3.5) [ 1693 ]

VOPISCUS (FLAVIUS).

*See* HISTORIÆ Augustæ scriptores. FL. VOPISCUS.

WILSON (ROBERT THOMAS)

History of the British expedition to Egypt; to which is subjoined, a sketch of the present state of that country and its means of defence. Illustrated with maps, and a portrait of Sir Ralph Abercromby. By ROBERT THOMAS WILSON, . . . V. 1, 2. *** The fourth edition. *London*, 1803. 8° (5.7×3.3) [ 2053 ]

WOLLSTONECRAFT (MARY), *afterwards Mrs. Godwin.*

An historical and moral view of the origin and progress of the French revolution; and the effect it has produced in Europe. By MARY WOLLSTONECRAFT. V. 1.
*London*, 1794. 8° (6×3.3) [ 1687 ]

YALE COLLEGE, *New Haven, Conn.*

Catalogue of books in the library of YALE COLLEGE. [*Classed.*]
*New Haven*, 1823. 8° (6.6×3.6) [ 502 ]

Catalogue of the library of the Linonian society, YALE COLLEGE, November, 1846. [*Alphabetical, with a classed index.*]
*New Haven*, 1846. 8° (6.5×4) [ 457 ]

Catalogue of the library of the society of Brothers in unity, YALE COLLEGE, April 1846. [*Alphabetical, with a classed index.*]
*New Haven*, 1846. 8° (6.7×3.8) [ 458 ]

# INDEX OF SUBJECTS.


**Antiquities.**
Dissertation on, *Voltaire.*
Grecian A. *See* GREECE.

**Athens.**
Rise and fall of, *Lytton.*

**Autobiography.**
Collection of lives. *Autobiography.*
A. of W. Jerdan. *Jerdan.*

**Bibliography.**
Bibliomania, or book-madness. *Dibdin.*
Catal. de livr. difficiles à trouver. *Clément.*
Dansk-norsk hist. Bibliothek. *Baden.*
Litteraturlexicon for Danmark, Norge og Island. *Nyerup.*
Bibliotheca Grenvilliana. *Grenville.*
Om Bibliotheksvidenskab. *Molbech.*
Ueber Bibliothekswissenschaft. *Molbech.*
Works in refutation of Methodism. *Decanver.*
*See* CATALOGUES.

**Bibliomania.**
Bibliomania, or book-madness. *Dibdin.*

**Biography.**
B. of classic authors. *Harwood.*
Celebrated characters of the French revol. *Ess.*
De vitis, etc. philosophorum. *Diogenes Laërtius.*
Lives of the Scotish poets. *Irving (D.).*
the United Irishmen. *Madden.*
twelve eminent judges. *Townsend.*
Sketches of living notables, in 1852. *Men.*
Staatkundig Nederland. *Scheltema.*
De rebus gestis Alexandri. *Curtius Rufus.*
Hist. de Christine, de Suède. *Catteau-Calleville.*
Napoléon. *Norvins.*
La défence de Marie de Médicis. *Morgues.*
La minorité de Louis XIV. *La Rochefoucauld.*
Life of Belisarius. *Stanhope.*
Chev. Bayard. *Simms.*
Dumouriez. *Dumouriez.*
Guicciardini. *Guicciardini.*
Julian. *La Bletterie.*
Napoleon. *Ess.*
Turenne. *Du Buisson.*
Lives of Haydn and Mozart, with observ. on Metastasio. *Bombet.*
Mém. de F. Dusson. *La Troussière.*
la comtesse de Murat. *M * * *.*
M. de Bordeaux. *C. (M. G. D.).*
Mem. of Cuvier. *Lee.*
J. d'Arc. *Arc.*
Political B. of L'd G. Bentinck. *Disraeli (B.).*
Reminiscences of M. Kelly. *Kelly.*
Vida de J. de Castro. *Freire de Andrade.*
Vie d'O. Maldachini. *Gualdi.*
Vie privée du cardinal Dubois. *Dubois.*

**Botany.**
Transactions of the Linnean soc. *Linnean soc.*
Trees and shrubs of Mass. *Massachusetts.*

**Catalogues.**
C. de livres difficiles à trouver. *Clément.*
C. of Bodleian libr'y. *Univ. of Oxford.*
C. of libr'y of Brothers in unity. *Yale college.*
C. of libr'y of Linonian soc. *Yale college.*
C. of libr'y of S. Parr. *Parr.*
C. of libr'y of T. Grenville. *Grenville.*
C. of libr'y of Yale college. *Yale college.*
C. of London libr'y. *London library.*

**Corfu.**
History of, *Jervis.*

**Denmark.**
Dansk-norsk hist. Bibliothek. *Baden.*
Forelaesninger over den danske Poesie. *Molbech.*
Litteraturlexicon for, *Nyerup.*
Udsigt over den danske Litteratur. *Thorsten.*

**Drama.**
Catal. of books on the British, *Univ. of Oxford.*
Diss. on the early Scotish, *Irving (D.).*

**Egypt.**
Br. expedition to, and present state of, *Wilson.*

**England.**
Br. expedition to Egypt. *Wilson.*
History of, *Graham.*
" *Hume.*
Hist. of E. and Scotland to the union. *Ayscu.*
Lives of twelve eminent judges. *Townsend.*
Sketches of the literature of, *Balfour.*
" " *Disraeli (I.).*
State papers: Henry VIII. *Great Britain.*
*See* GREAT BRITAIN.

**Europe.**
Manual of the geogr. and hist. of, *Ungewitter.*

**France.**
Celebrated characters of the revol. *Ess.*
De la révolution françoise. *Necker.*
Hist. des instit. representitives. *Thibaudeau.*
Hist. of the restoration. *Lamartine.*
Mémoires sur le consulat. *Mémoires.*
Mem. and times of J. d'Arc. *Arc.*
State of music in, *Bombet.*
View of the revol. *Wollstonecraft.*

**Geography.**
Manual of European, *Ungewitter.*

**Germany.**
Germania. *Tacitus.*
Geschichte des deutschen Volkes. *Luden.*

**Granada.**
Conquest of, *Irving (W.).*

**Great Britain.**
Catal. of books on Br. drama. *Univ. of Oxford.*
Catal. of books on Br. topogr. *Univ. of Oxford.*
Catal. of Br. birds. *Eyton.*
Hist. of Br. birds. *Eyton.*
*See* ENGLAND, IRELAND and SCOTLAND.

**Greece.**
Antiquities of. *Potter.*
Hist. of Corfu and the Ionian repub. *Jervis.*
Recueil de cartes, etc. *Barbié du Bocage.*
Voyage d'Anacharsis. *Barthélemy.*

**Hebrews.**
*See* JEWS.

**History.**
Histoire universelle. *Bossuet.*
Manual of European, *Ungewitter.*
Orosii historiographi opus. *Orosius.*
Philosophy of, *Voltaire.*
Recherches sur l'hist. ancienne. *Volney.*

**Holland.**
*See* NETHERLANDS.

**Iceland.**
Litteraturlexicon for, *Nyerup.*

**India.**
Oriental hist. mss. *Oriental.*

**Ionian Islands.**
Hist. of the republic of, *Jervis.*

**Ireland.**
Ancient histories of. *Ancient.*
United Irishmen; their lives and times. *Madden.*
*See* GREAT BRITAIN.

**Italy.**
History of, *Guicciardini.*
I. avant il dominio dei Romani. *Micali.*
State of music in, *Bombet.*

**Java.**
History of, *Raffles.*

**Jews.**
History of, *Basnage de Beauval.*

**Libraries.**
Catalogues of L. *See* CATALOGUES.
Om Bibliotheksvidenskap. *Molbech.*
Ueber Bibliothekswissenschaft. *Molbech.*

**Literature.**
Catal. of books on Saxon and northern, *Univ. of Oxford.*
Curiosities of, *Disraeli (I.).*
Literary hist. of Scotland. *Irving (D.).*
Sketches of English, *Balfour.*
" " *Disraeli (I.).*
View of Athenian, *Lytton.*
Udsigt over den danske, *Thorsten.*

**Methodism.**
Works in refutation of, *Decanver.*

**Music.**
State of M. in France and Italy. *Bombet.*

**Mythology.**
Ad Apollodori bibliothecam notæ. *Heyne.*
Apollodori bibliotheca. *Apollodorus.*
Historiæ poeticæ scriptores. *Gale.*

**Natural History.**
Plinii historia naturalis. *Plinius Secundus.*
*See* BOTANY, ORNITHOLOGY and ZOOLOGY.

**Netherlands.**
Staatkundig N.; biogr. kaart. *Scheltema.*

**Northern Literature.**
Catal. of books on, *Univ. of Oxford.*

**Norway.**
Dansk-norsk hist. Bibliothek. *Baden.*
Litteraturlexicon for, *Nyerup.*

**Ornithology.**
Catal. of British birds. *Eyton.*
Hist. of British birds. *Eyton.*

**Painting.**
Het groot schilderboek. *Lairesse.*

**Pharmacy.**
Homish apothecarye booke. *Most.*

**Philosophers.**
De vitis, etc. philosophorum. *Diogenes Laërtius.*

**Philosophy.**
View of Athenian, *Lytton.*

**Poetry.**
Forelæsninger over den danske, *Molbech.*
Catal. of early English, *Univ. of Oxford.*

**Portugal.**
Historia de, *Herculano.*

**Prussia.**
Hist. secrète de la cour de Berlin. *Riqueti.*
Secret hist. of the court of Berlin. *Riqueti.*

**Reviews, Literary.**
American quarterly, *American.*
Edinburgh, *Edinburgh.*
Monthly, *Monthly.*
North American, *North American.*

**Rome.**
Civil and constitutional hist. of, *Bankes.*
Elements of the hist. of, *Cobbett.*
Gallus: or, Rom. scenes. *Becker.*
Historiæ. *Paterculus.*
Historiæ Augustæ scriptores. *Historiæ.*
Méthode pour apprendre l'hist. rom. *Méthode.*
Method of learning Rom. hist. *Méthode.*
Taciti opera. *Tacitus.*

**Saxon Literature.**
Catal. of books on, *Univ. of Oxford.*

**Scotland.**
Literary hist. and drama of, *Irving (D.).*
Hist. of England and S. to the union. *Ayscu.*
*See* GREAT BRITAIN.

**Spain.**
Hist. de la revolucion de, *Queypo de Llano.*
Hist. of the war of succession in, *Stanhope.*

**Sweden.**
Précis historique de, *Catteau-Calleville.*

**Theatre.**
Acc't of King's theatre, London. *Kelly.*

**Topography.**
Catal. of books on British, *Univ. of Oxford.*

**War, Art of.**
Astutie militari. *Frontinus.*
Précis des guerres de César. *Napoléon.*
Strategematica. *Frontinus.*

**Zoology.**
Zoological journal. *Bell.*

# EXPLANATIONS OF INITIALS

USED IN THE LOCAL INDEX.

---

A. L., *for* ASTOR LIBRARY.
B. A., *for* BOSTON ATHENEUM.
B. U., *for* BROWN UNIVERSITY.
C. H. S., *for* CAMBRIDGE HIGH SCHOOL.
H. C., *for* HARVARD COLLEGE.
L. C., *for* LIBRARY OF CONGRESS.
L. C. P., *for* LIBRARY COMPANY OF PHILADELPHIA.
L. S., *for* LANE SEMINARY.
N. Y. S. L., *for* NEW YORK STATE LIBRARY.
S. C. C., *for* SOUTH CAROLINA COLLEGE.
S. I., *for* SMITHSONIAN INSTITUTION.
U. A., *for* UNIVERSITY OF ALABAMA.
Y. C., *for* YALE COLLEGE.

# LOCAL INDEX.


| No. | Index |
|---|---|
| 140 | A. L., B. U., S. I. |
| 141 | A. L., B. U., S. I. |
| 142 | A. L., B. U., S. I. |
| 144 | A. L., B. U., S. I. |
| 145 | A. L., B. U., S. I. |
| 216 | B. A., H. C., S. I., Y. C. |
| 290 | L. C. P., S. I., Y. C. |
| 291 | L. S., S. I., Y. C. |
| 292 | H. C., S. C. C., S. I. |
| 310 | S. I., U. A., Y. C. |
| 317 | A. L., S. I. |
| 391 | B. U., S. I. |
| 457 | A. L., S. I. |
| 458 | L. S., S. I. |
| 502 | S. I., Y. C. |
| 644 | A. L., S. I. |
| 645 | B. U., S. I. |
| 1002 | H. C., L. C., U. A. |
| 1004 | L. C., Y. C. |
| 1006 | B. A., L. C. |
| 1019 | C. H. S., L. C., S. C. C. |
| 1020 | L. C., S. C. C. |
| 1029 | L. C., U. A. |
| 1053 | L. C., P. L. C. |
| 1054 | A. L., L. C. |
| 1069 | B. A., L. C., N. Y. S. L. |
| 1070 | L. C., L. S. |
| 1114 | H. C., L. C., L. C. P. |
| 1147 | B. U., L. C., U. A., Y. C. |
| 1154 | L. C., S. I. |
| 1162 | B. U., L. C., Y. C. |
| 1201 | L. C., N. Y. S. L., U. A. |
| 1202 | A. L., C. H. S., L. C. |
| 1215 | L. C., L. S. |
| 1216 | L. C., Y. C. |
| 1255 | H. C., L. C., S. I. |
| 1256 | C. H. S., L. C., U. A. |
| 1257 | A. L., L. C., L. C. P. |
| 1258 | L. C. |
| 1259 | L. C., N. Y. S. L. |
| 1278 | B. A., L. C. |
| 1288 | B. U., L. C. |
| 1304 | H. C., L. C., U. A. |
| 1377 | B. A., L. C., Y. C. |
| 1378 | H. C., L. C., S. C. C. |
| 1379 | L. C., S. I. |
| 1384 | L. S., L. C., S. C. C. |
| 1410 | L. C., Y. C. |
| 1414 | A. L., L. C., S. C. C. |
| 1427 | H. C., L. C., U. A. |
| 1429 | L. C., L. S. |
| 1435 | B. U., C. H. S., L. C. |
| 1436 | H. C., L. C. |
| 1489 | A. L., C. H. S., L. C. |
| 1490 | L. C., L. C. P. |
| 1529 | L. C., N. Y. S. L. |
| 1584 | A. L., B. U., L. C., Y. C. |
| 1596 | C. H. S., L. C. |
| 1600 | L. C., S. C. C. |
| 1621 | L. C., U. A. |
| 1630 | B. U., L. C. |
| 1687 | L. C., L. C. P. |
| 1693 | L. C., N. Y. S. L. |
| 1702 | H. C., L. C., Y. C. |
| 1707 | C. H. S., L. C. |
| 1710 | A. L., L. C., L. S. |
| 1719 | B. A., H. C., L. C. |
| 1720 | L. C., S. I. |
| 1721 | L. C., U. A. |
| 1723 | B. U., L. C., Y. C. |
| 1748 | C. H. S., H. C., L. C. |
| 1771 | L. C., S. C. C. |
| 1775 | L. C., N. Y. S. L. |
| 1815 | A. L., L. C., S. I. |
| 1816 | C. H. S., L. C., S. I. |
| 1828 | A. L., H. C., L. C. |
| 1854 | B. U., L. C., S. I. |
| 1858 | L. C., L. S. |

| | | | |
|---|---|---|---|
| 1864 | H. C., L. C., N. Y. S. S. | 2631 | L. C., S. I. |
| 1876 | L. C., S. C. C., U. A. | 2638 | H. C., L. C. |
| 1948 | L. C., L. C. P. | 2646 | B. U., L. C., S. I. |
| 1967 | L. C., L. S. | 2659 | C. H. S., L. C., S. C. C. |
| 2003 | B. A., L. C., Y. C. | 2700 | C. H. S., L. C., Y. C. |
| 2005 | C. H. S., L. C. | 2707 | A. L., L. C., S. I. |
| 2039 | H. C., L. C. | 2711 | B. A., C. H. S., L. C. |
| 2040 | L. C., N. Y. S. L. | 2728 | H. C., L. C. |
| 2053 | L. C., S. C. C., U. A. | 2729 | B. U., H. C., L. C. |
| 2070 | A. L., L. C., Y. C. | 2731 | A. L., L. C., U. A. |
| 2099 | B. U., L. C., U. A. | 2733 | L. C., L. C. P. |
| 2118 | C. H. S., L. C. | 2734 | B. A., B. U., L. C., S. C. C. |
| 2119 | L. C., L. S., Y. C. | 2736 | C. H. S., L. C. |
| 2156 | L. C., S. C. C., Y. C. | 2737 | L. C., N. Y. S. L. |
| 2219 | L. C., S. I., U. A. | 2738 | L. C., L. S. |
| 2273 | H. C., L. C., Y. C. | 2742 | L. C., S. I. |
| 2274 | H. O., L. C., Y. C. | 2757 | A. L., L. C., Y. C. |
| 2275 | H. C., L. C., Y. C. | 2771 | H. C., L. C., S. C. C. |
| 2276 | H. C., L. C., Y. C. | 2778 | L. C., U. A. |
| 2296 | B. A., L. C. | 2779 | B. U., L. C., N. Y. S. L. |
| 2332 | L. C., U. A. | 2780 | B. A., L. C., U. A. |
| 2424 | A. L., L. C., L. C. P. | 2781 | B. A., L. C., S. I. |
| 2425 | L. C., L. C. P., U. A. | 2782 | A. L., L. C., S. I. |
| 2426 | H. C., L. C., Y. C. | 2783 | L. C., S. I., Y. C. |
| 2427 | B. A., L. C. | 2784 | B. U., L. C., S. I. |
| 2428 | L. C., N. Y. S. L., S. I. | 2789 | L. C., L. S. |
| 2440 | B. U., L. C. | 2790 | A. L., C. H. S., L. C. |
| 2441 | C. H. S., L. C., U. A. | 2791 | L. C., N. Y. S. L. |
| 2442 | B. U., L. C., S. C. C. | 2806 | A. L., L. C., S. C. C. |
| 2455 | B. U., L. C., L. C. P. | 2825 | B. A., L. C. |
| 2479 | Y. C., L. C., L. S. | 2851 | B. U., L. C., L. S. |
| 2556 | L. C., U. A. | 2893 | L. C., N. Y. S. L. |
| 2622 | A. L., L. C. | 2894 | L. C., N. Y. S. L. |
| 2629 | A. L., L. C. | 2940 | L. C., S. I., Y. C. |
| 2630 | L. C. | | |

www.ingramcontent.com/pod-product-compliance
Lightning Source LLC
LaVergne TN
LVHW021429110826
845150LV00007B/2147

* 9 7 8 1 4 2 5 5 0 7 3 8 1 *